theTofu Cookbook

the Tofu Cookbook

Cathy Bauer & Juel Andersen

Woodcuts by David Frampton

 Rodale Press, Emmaus, Pennsylvania

Book design by Barbara Field

Printed in the United States of America on recycled paper, containing a high percentage of de-inked fiber.

Library of Congress Cataloging in Publication Data

Bauer, Cathy.
    The tofu cookbook.
    Includes index.
    1. Cookery (Bean curd)   I. Andersen, Juel, joint author. II. Title.
TX814.5.B4B38   641.6'5'655   79-9709
 ISBN 0-87857-246-5 paperback

The lowest figure indicates the number of this printing:

4 6 8 10 9 7 5 paperback

We dedicate this book to all those who have tried tofu—once.

Contents

Recipes in This Book xi

1
What Is Tofu? 1

2
Getting Better Acquainted 5
  Saving money with tofu 5
  A waste of land 6
  Tofu and better nutrition 6
  Growing your own 9

3
Making Tofu 12
  The equipment 12
  The solidifier 14
  The process 15
  Making tofu in quantity 19

4
Using Tofu 22
  Fresh tofu 22

How to revive aging tofu 23
Making firmer tofu 23
Freezing it 23
Serving it plain and simple 24
Tofu for vegetarians 24
Tofu for dieters 25
Becoming an innovator 26

5
Okara and Whey 29
  Okara 29
  Whey 31

6
Soymilk 35
  Soymilk recipes in this book 36
  How to make it 36
  Koumiss 38
  Milkshakes 39

7
Processed Soy Protein (PSP) 41
  What is Processed Soy Protein? 41
  PSP recipes in this book 43

THE RECIPES

8
Main Dishes 45

9
Side Dishes and Preparations 83

10
Soup, Sandwich, and Salad 94

11
Baking with Okara: Bread, Crackers, and Pastries 109

12
Sauces, Dips, and Spreads 127

13
Breakfasts 140

14
Desserts: Pies, Cakes, Cookies, and Assorted Fancies 149

15
Kids' Specials and Baby Food 161

Appendices
  A Substituting flours 171
  B Composition of spices 172
  C Miscellaneous substitutions 173
  D Table of equivalents 174
  E Fahrenheit and Celsius equivalents 175
  F Recommended daily dietary allowances 176

Index 178

Salt is optional or missing in most of the recipes in this book. The body's need for salt is ordinarily met by the natural sodium content of foods. By salting food in cooking and again at the table, you are adding more salt than your body needs, with a risk to health. Stop and think before you salt.

Recipes in This Book

Main Dishes

Tofu Lasagna	47
Baked Stuffed Zucchini	47
Broiled Tofu Slices	48
Deep-Fried Sesame Tofu	49
Ravioli	50
Cheese Rarebit	51
Tofu Broccoli Casserole	51
Eggplant Casserole Italienne	52
Potato–Tofu–Cabbage Casserole	53
Tuna Tofu Casserole	53
Tofu Artichoke Casserole with Chicken or Tuna	54
Tortilla Casserole	55
Garbanzo Okara Loaf	55
Tofu Meat Loaf	56
Carrot Tofu Loaf	56
Carrots Parmesan with Tofu	57
Meatless Chili	57
Hot Tofu Tuna Salad	58
Corn and Tofu Soufflé	59
Spinach Soufflé	60
Vegetable Soufflé	60

Okara Zucchini Soufflé 61
Zucchini Entrée Squares 61
Lentil Stew 62
Kima (Indian Curry) 62
Tofu Enchiladas 63
Enchilada Sauce 63
Mushrooms à la Crème Tofu 64
Shrimp and Tofu 65
Okara–Mushroom–Shrimp Curry Patties 66
Tofu à la Newburg 66
Tofu Noodles Romanov 67
Almond–Vegetable–Tofu Sauté 67
Dow-Foo Chow Yoke (Stir-Fried Tofu).............................. 68
Tamale Pie 68
Okara Meat Croquettes 69
Tofu Quiche 70
Vegetable Quiche 71
Pie Shell for Quiche 71
Green Peppers Stuffed with Tofu 72
Using Homemade PSP 73
Dinner Loaf with PSP 74
PSP Sloppy Joes 74
Stuffed Cabbage Rolls 75
Tacos 76
Carrot Tofu Loaf with PSP 76
Chili Con PSP 77
Spaghetti Sauce 78
PSP Stroganoff 78
Japanese-Style Meatballs 79
PSP Burgers 79
Skillet Supper 80
Stuffed Grape Leaves (Dolmadakia) 80
Pizza Dough with Okara 82
Pizza Sauce 82

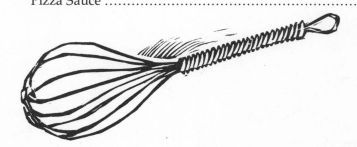

Side Dishes and Preparations

Tiropeta (Greek Cheese Pie) 84
Kreplach or Pierogi 84
Okara Turkey Dumplings 85
Chinese Steamed Buns (Pao-Tze) 85
Okara Stuffing for Poultry 86
PSP Snack 86
Batter for Deep Frying 87
Okara Fry-and-Bake Coating 87
Tofu Cheese Ball 88
Filled Puffs (Brandteigkrapfer mit Salziger Fulle) 88
Rebaked Potatoes with Tofu 89
Spiked Popcorn 90
Egg Roll 90
Wonton or Pot Sticker Dough (Whole Wheat Egg Noodles) 91
Pot Stickers (Kuo Teh) 92
Wonton 93

Soup, Sandwich, and Salad

Minestrone 96
Basic Cream Soup 97
Ukranian Borscht 97
Chicken Soup or Broth 98
Clam Chowder with PSP 98
Vegetarian Potato Soup 99

Gazpacho 99
Grilled Cheese and Tofu Sandwich 100
Tofu Tuna Salad Sandwich 100
Tofu in Sandwiches 100
Tia's Tofu Sandwich 101
Waldorf Salad 101
Uncle Perk's Potato Salad 102
Sweet and Sour Salad 102
Tofu–Egg Salad 103
Tabouli (Bulgur Salad) 103
Spinach Salad 104
Oriental Salad and Dressing 104
Tofu Mayonnaise 105
Tomato Dressing 106
Tarragon Tofu Dressing 106
Tofu Dressing Extraordinaire 106
Tofu–Blue Cheese Dressing 107
French Dressing 107
Tofu Tahini Salad Dressing 107
Green Goddess Dressing 108
Low-Calorie Thousand Island Dressing 108

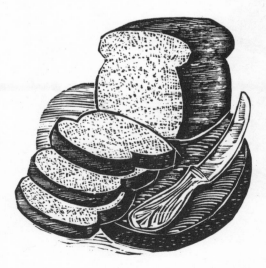

Baking with Okara: Bread, Crackers, and Pastries

Rye Bread Sticks 111
English Muffins 111
Mugs' and Kate's Pincushion Rolls 112

Okara Danish Yeast Dough 112
Buttermilk Kuchen 113
Whole Wheat Sesame Buns and Bread 114
Orange Nut Bread 115
Sourdough Health Bread 115
Sourdough Starter 116
Peasant Bread 116
Anadama Bread 117
Irish Soda Bread 117
Nellie Twomey's Soda Bread 118
Wheatless, Eggless, Milkless Fruit Bread 119
Pumpkin Spice Bread 119
Banana–Coconut–Tofu Bread (Eggless) 120
Banana Okara Bread 120
Casserole Dill Bread 121
Quick Coffee Cake 121
Scones with Okara 122
Okara Cornsticks 123
Okara Bran Biscuits 123
Buttermilk Doughnuts 124
Oatmeal Crackers with Tofu 124
Tofu Okara Crackers 125
Okara Flatbread 126

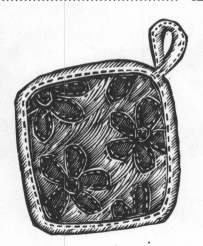

Sauces, Dips, and Spreads

Basic White Sauce 129
Basic White Sauce from Stock (Velouté) 129
Tofu Hollandaise Sauce 131

Tofu Bearnaise Sauce 132
Ymer (with Tofu) 132
Creamy Tofu Mustard Sauce 133
Tomato Sauce 133
Sweet Yogurt Sauce 133
Fish-Flavored Sauce 134
Curry Sauce 134
Dipping Sauces for Tofu Cubes 135
Tofu Dip Base 136
Dip for Vegetables 136
Liptauer (An Austrian Dip or Spread) 137
Tofu Ghenouj 137
Tofu Cream Cheese 138
Cucumber Sandwich Spread 138
Seafood Spread 139
Blue Cheese Spread 139

Breakfasts

Klondike Pancakes 141
Persian Pancakes 141
Æbleskiver (Spherical Danish Pancakes) 142
Okara Sourdough Pancakes and Waffles 143
Dieter's Pancakes 144
Okara Whole Wheat Waffles 144

Rice Flour–Okara Waffles 145
Scrambled Tofu (with or without Eggs) 145
Cornmeal Cereal 146
French Toast 147
Risengrød (Rice Cooked in Milk) 147
Okara Sausage Patties 148

Desserts: Pies, Cakes, Cookies, and Assorted Fancies

Tofu Cheese Pie 150
Yogurt Pie (Yiaourtopeta) 151
Eggless Lemon Pie 151
Sweet Pie Shell 152
Tofu Cheese Torte 152
Hazelnut Okara Torte 153
Basic Soy Custard (Baked) 153
Eggnog Mousse (Bavarian Cream) 154
Spanish Creme 155
Basic Mousse 155
Fudge Brownies 156
Oatmeal Okara Cookies 156
Okara and Coconut Macaroons 157
Zucchini Cookies 157
Okara Tofu Spice Bars (Eggless) 158
Fruit Dumplings 159
Okara Carrot Cake 159
Okara Blueberry Cake 160

xvii

Kids' Specials and Baby Food
Glorious Mess 163
Fantastic Island Soup 163
Tofu Toybox 164
Ms. Muffett Soup 165
Whey Soup 165
Carrot and Tofu Salad 165
Red, White, and Brown Rounds 165
Tofu Smoothie 166
Soy Shake 166
Coconut Mothballs 166
Old Cake Cookies 167
Frisbee® Cookies 167
Michelle's Mud Pies 168
Baby Cereal 168
Baby Stew or Soup 169
Baby Vegetable 169
Baby Fruit 170

Acknowledgments

It has been three years since I began my love affair with tofu. Along the way to publication of this book there have been many frustrations and problems including many burned batches of tofu. But it has been a wonderful experience. There are people who have helped in many ways, small and large, and I want to say thank you to them.

Thank you to John, my patient and supportive husband, who has lent his indulgence, encouragement, and acceptance to my work—to say nothing of his having offered his digestion to a thousand and one concoctions that were entirely alien to his Danish food predilections.

Thank you to Sigrid Antonia, my lovely daughter, who joined her father as a private taster. She also helped by designing a few recipes on her own.

I thank my husband, again, for providing me with a hideaway in which to work and for putting up with my long absences while I was writing. And my thanks to Malcolm Bauer for being handy when my chimney got stopped up and when the pipes froze. He is responsible for a few recipes.

To my coauthor my debt is obvious. With her assistance in the writing, I was freer to develop and test recipes.

To Bill Shurtleff and Akiko Aoyagi, authors of *The Book of Tofu* (Westminster, Md.: Autumn Press, 1977), I offer a small Oriental bow of respect for their encouragement and for their definitive book.

And finally, thank you to Roger B. Yepsen, Jr., our editor at Rodale Press, for not hanging up on me during endless telephone conversations. He has helped make a dream a reality.

Juel Andersen

What
Is Tofu? 1

What is tofu? The synonyms soy cheese and bean curd suggest the answer: tofu is a high-protein, cholesterol-free food made by solidifying soymilk. It might strike you as an unfamiliar dairy cheese in consistency and color, but this Eastern staple has its very own mild flavor.

Tofu looks strange to the unfamiliar eye. Most people know it only as an Oriental curiosity, something to stir around in a wok. This book was written with the aim of making tofu an everyday staple in your kitchen. Tofu is a food whose time has come. It has already begun to catch on outside of Chinatown, appearing in co-ops, natural food stores, and now supermarkets as well.

Tofu is catching on in the Western world because of changes in the way we eat. Many of us need to alter our diets, as evidenced by obesity, and by the way heart disease, digestive disorders, and arteriosclerosis are pruning our life spans. We are learning that meat need not be the keystone of nutrition.

Food shoppers are more sophisticated now; they no longer associate protein with the meat counter. In comparing tofu with two popular sources of protein, hamburger and cheddar cheese, a table says it simplest. The figures below are for four ounces of each food, the meat being raw. Two figures are given for hamburger, representing an extra-lean cut with 10 percent fat and a cut the butcher calls "lean" but contains 21 percent fat.

Table 1
Protein and calorie figures for 4 ounces (approximately an average serving) of three high-protein foods

	Protein (gr.)	Calories (gr.)	Calories per gr. of protein
Cheddar cheese	28	451	16
Ground beef			
10% fat	23.5	203	9
21% fat	20	304	15
Tofu	9	82	9

Price is another reason tofu is becoming more popular in the West. Although the prices of all goods and services have blossomed with inflation, cheap food strikes us as an inalienable right. Well, you needn't spend a huge chunk of your weekly wage on meat and cheese and fish—soybeans are still cheap and, as Chapter 4 relates, making tofu at home is a steamy but pleasant process. (And fresh tofu beats store-bought. Make it yourself, and you'll come to know the shy but personable flavor of soy cheese.) Homemade tofu can cost less than 25 cents per pound. If somebody else makes it, naturally you'll pay more.

Not only is tofu good for you and relatively inexpensive, but it further obliges us by being easy to digest. Many folks, young and old, cannot eat dairy foods. For them, tofu and soymilk can be a blessing. And many of us who can eat dairy foods might be better off with fewer animal fats from these foods. Through this book, you can learn to make a number of creamy dishes, sauces, and desserts without the heaviness and indigestibility of cream and cheese.

There are other problems with meat and dairy products. Shoppers are increasingly suspect of additives in their food, studying the small print that admits the use of chemical stabilizers, flavor enhancers, and preservatives. But we have no label to tell us what was fed and injected into the animal that provided the meat or milk. Soybeans, sitting down at the low end of the food chain, miss out on all sorts of chemicals that are absorbed and concentrated by animals, to be passed on to us in their flesh and milk. While there may be no longer such a thing as pure, pristine food, eaters of soyfoods have some comfort in knowing they're eating as sanely as they can.

You can't eat moral issues, but some tofu fans also take comfort in knowing that their meals don't require an enormous investment in land and fertilizers. The figures vary, depending on who you listen to, but one figure often given is 20. Twenty soy eaters can be fed from the land it takes to feed one meat eater. Put another way, a portion of beef takes 20 times the land needed to produce a portion of soyfood, protein for protein. It is naive to believe that your decision to keep the sirloin in the freezer and eat tofu tonight will enable 19 malnourished people to eat. But the sheer enormity of that figure, 20, makes soyfoods more attractive for some.

Tofu couldn't play a big role in the American diet if its taste came through like liver and onions, day after day—it's impossible to get tired of tofu because it can take on many forms and an infinite number of flavors. Served plain, in a salad or soup perhaps, it reminds one of a mild cheese. When broiled, it becomes quite meatlike. Freeze tofu and the resulting product is surprisingly chewy. A blender transforms this food into rich-tasting sauces or creamy salad dressings. And tofu picks up the taste and aroma of whatever accompanies it into the pot, pan, or casserole dish.

With the recipes in this book, you can continue enjoying the flavors you like best while saving money, cutting down on cholesterol and calories, and avoiding the noxious additives found in processed foods. Supplement your favorite lasagna recipe with tofu, and you get by with less ricotta and little or no meat. The dish will be just as tasty, and even more satisfying because of its lightness. Mix in tofu the next time you scramble some eggs. Again, you'll have a lighter version of a familiar food—a boon to anyone concerned with their weight or cholesterol intake.

An important advantage to making your own tofu is that you end up with not only the product itself but two worthy by-products—okara and whey. Okara is the pulp left behind after soymilk has been pressed from the bean. It is white, fibrous, and contains 3 or 4 percent protein by weight. Used in baked goods, okara contributes fiber, protein, and improved texture. It also serves as a meat extender, in dinner loaves and patties.

Whey is the clear liquid left behind when soymilk is solidified into tofu. It too offers a share of the bean's protein, though not as much as okara. The brave can drink whey straight as a tea; the thrifty can follow Japanese tradition and make use of its mild lathering property for washing the tofu-making utensils. But most of us would rather put it to use as a nutritious soup stock.

On the way to making tofu, another valuable food is produced: soymilk. Use soymilk instead of dairy milk in your favorite recipes, cup for cup.

If tofu is so great, then how come we aren't all eating it? Well, skeptical reader, keep in mind that pizza didn't catch on in this country until the men came home from Italy after the Second World War. But tofu has an image problem. The name is funny (though no more so than pizza, really), and it's associated with Oriental foods. The American view of foreign cuisine is very simplistic. A couple of a country's dishes are appropriated, and the rest forgotten. Our misconceptions know no boundaries. The Italians gorge themselves on pasta, the Mexicans live on tacos, the Indians dump curry on everything, an Englishman will only eat meat if it's well boiled, and an Oriental—well, we all like to poke around with chopsticks as if our hands had contracted a spontaneous palsy, but on the way home from the restaurant you've got nothing but an empty stomach, a fortune cookie, and an MSG hangover.

But tofu deserves a chance to make it in the American kitchen. As in things spiritual and medical, the East has something to teach the West about food. A suggested title for this book was *The Americanization of Tofu,* for that is what these pages are all about—taking an unfamiliar food and showing how it can star in hundreds of conventionally delicious recipes, including soufflés, quiches, crepes, pancakes, sandwiches, sauces, beverages, breads, salads, soups, and a good selection of desserts. Tofu can find its way into breakfast, lunch, dinner, and in-between-meal snacks.

Getting Better Acquainted 2

Now that you know what tofu is and have learned something of its potential, here's a look at how it compares to more conventional foods in terms of economy, efficiency of land use, and nutritional value. We'll even give you a few suggestions on growing your own beans in the backyard.

Saving money with tofu

As tofu becomes more popular, it is suffering the fate of other natural foods, unprocessed bran, for example. Natural foods such as these are perverted by conventional producers, who repackage and often adulterate the basic product, and then charge an inflated price. You may have seen tofu selling for well over $1 a pound. And you may have noticed chemical ingredients are being slipped into this previously quick-spoiling product to increase its shelf life. Don't be put off by the mention of solidifiers, such as calcium sulfate, calcium chloride, magnesium chloride, or nigari; these natural compounds are nutritionally valuable. Preservatives give tofu a sour taste that can be immediately detected.

If you don't want to pay the going price for commercial tofu, try making your own. You'll be astonished at just how cheap this is.

From a pound of soybeans (which costs, at this writing, about 35 cents) you can make about 2½ pounds of tofu with its attendant free by-products, okara and whey. Or you can cut the tofu-making process short and come up with almost 2 gallons of soymilk and still have lots of okara. This translates to about 15 cents per pound for tofu and about 5 cents a quart for soymilk.

Fresh soymilk is one of the best things about making your own tofu. The difference between fresh soymilk and that made from powders or soy flour is enormous. You can use soymilk interchangeably with cow's milk. In cooking, the bean milk will be indistinguishable.

A waste of land

The affluent countries of the world seem to base their food production on waste. We feed as much as 21 pounds of high-protein feed (such as soybeans) to cattle to produce a single pound of beef. As Frances Moore Lappé writes in her landmark book, *Diet for a Small Planet* (New York: Ballantine, 1971), we have created "protein factories in reverse." We feed proteins to animals in great quantities to get a fraction of that protein back in the form of meat. That same 21 pounds of soybeans could be used to make about 53 pounds of tofu or 168 quarts of soymilk, providing the recommended allowance of protein for 34 people instead of just one.

Tofu and better nutrition

Many in the Western world gorge themselves with meat, believing that if some protein is good, more has got to be better. It's true that we must consume protein, because without it the body is unable to synthesize 8 of the 22 proteins or amino acids necessary to life. The *essential amino acids* are found in rich amounts in legumes, nuts, and seeds, and in cereal grains, as well as in animal products. The array of amino acids is not complete in any plant food, so it is necessary to eat more than one vegetable protein source at any given meal in order to satisfy the need for protein. Combining proteins in this manner is known as *protein complementarity*. Traditional meals and dishes of people around the world answer this need for complementarity, combining seeds and beans, dairy goods and grains, and other groupings whose strengths and weaknesses mesh. Table 2 lists the amounts of essential amino acids found in tofu and several basic foods.

Table 2
Essential amino-acid content of tofu and complementary foods:

A means the amount is adequate;
M means the amount is marginal;
D means the amount is deficient.

	Isoleucine	Leucine	Lysine	Sulfur-containing (cystine and methionine)	Aromatic (phenylalanine and tyrosine)	Threonine	Tryptophan	Valine
Tofu	A	A	A	D	A+	A	A	A
Soymilk	A	A	M	D	A+	A	A	A
Brown rice	A	A	M	A	A+	M	A	A
Whole wheat flour	A	A	D	A	A	M	A	A
Sesame seeds	A+	A+	D	A	A+	A	A	A
Sunflower seeds	A+	A	D	D	A	A	A	A+
Cornmeal	A	A+	D	M	A	A	D	A
Peanuts	A	A	D	D	A+	A	A	A+
Cow's milk	A	A	A	D	A	A	A	A
Eggs	A	A	A	A	A	A	A	A
Salmon (silver and humpback)	A	M	A+	A	A	A	A	M
Chicken	A+	A	A+	A	A	M	A	D
Beef	A	A	A+	D	A	A	M	A
Kidney beans	A	A	A+	D	A+	A	A	A

(From "Food Composition Table for Use in East Asia." Food and Agriculture Organization of the United Nations, December 1972)

It is interesting to note in the table that, with the exception of eggs, there is no single food that supplies all the necessary amino acids in adequate amounts. All have deficiencies, even our hero, red meat.

By eating tofu with a whole grain bread, some nuts, or seeds, we can boost the total usable protein of a meal by as much as 40 percent. An important point is that the complementary foods must be eaten at the same meal for full benefit, and not at varying times during the day.

7

Such food combinations are very easy to plan in everyday meals. You might try tofu spreads on whole grain bread, stir-fried Asian dishes with brown rice, or tofu enchiladas with tortillas and seeds. A simple way to complement the protein of a tofu meal, or even a roast beef meal, is to have plenty of whole grain bread on hand to serve with it.

How much of each food should you eat for maximum benefit? Just allow reasonable helpings of each food group. It would be a trial and a bore to slavishly calculate for every meal.

Tofu offers minerals as well as protein—it's high in potassium and iron. When solidified with a calcium salt such as calcium sulfate or natural nigari, tofu contains more calcium than dairy milk.

Okara contains half the protein and fat of tofu (about 17 percent of the protein originally in the soybean). It is much higher in carbohydrates than tofu. The main contribution of okara to diet is fiber—an especially important factor in diets heavy on processed foods.

Whey ends up with a small percentage of the original protein in the soybean, but carries off most of the B vitamins, as these are water soluble. Whey is also rich in various natural sugars which give it a

Table 3
Composition of foods related to tofu and okara*†

100 gr. portions	Water (%)	Calories	Protein (gr.)	Fat (gr.)	Carbohydrates (gr.)	Fiber (gr.)	Calcium (mg.)
Beef hamburger (cooked), 20% fat	54	286	24	20	. . .	. . .	11
Tofu, 4% fat	85	72	7.8	4.2	2.4	0.1	128
Cow's milk, 3.7% fat	87	66	3.5	3.7	4.9	. . .	117
Soymilk, 1.5% fat	92	33	3.4	1.5	2.2	. . .	21
Cottage cheese, 4.2% fat	78	106	13.6	4.2	2.9	. . .	94
Okara, 1.5% fat	84	67	3.6	1.5	10.4	2.1	86
Eggs, 11.5% fat	74	163	13	11.5	0.9	. . .	54
Yogurt, 3.4% fat	88	62	3	3.4	4.9	. . .	111

*U.S. Department of Agriculture, *Nutritive Value of American Foods: In Common Units,* prepared by Catherine F. Adams (Washington, D.C.: Government Printing Office, 1975), p. 155.
†"Food Composition Table for Use in East Asia." Food and Agriculture Organization of the United Nations, December 1972.

sweet taste. Much of the solidifier salt remains in the whey, increasing its mineral content.

Growing your own

Some tofu afficionados grow their own beans for the satisfaction of controlling every step of the tofu-making process, from bean to finished cake. They also save money, and ensure that the beans are grown without chemical fertilizers or pesticides. And prudent gardening can produce beans with superior nutritive value.

You might also want to try cooking with soybeans in their fresh green state. Cooked just as they come from the garden, the beans are an excellent source of vitamin A (700 International Units per 100 grams, or 140 I.U. for the dried beans). Sprouted beans offer a good dose of vitamin C; surprisingly, the vitamin C content increases somewhat with refrigeration. They're also rich in vitamins E and K. It is important to remember that soy sprouts, being a raw soy product, should be cooked before eating if you wish to take advantage of their protein. You may find that sautéed sprouts have an improved flavor, as well.

100 gr. portions	Iron (mg.)	Sodium (mg.)	Potassium (mg.)	Vitamin A (I.U.)	Thiamine B_1 (mg.)	Riboflavin B_2 (mg.)	Niacin B_3 (mg.)	Vitamin C (mg.)
Beef hamburger (cooked), 20% fat	3.2	47	450	40	0.09	0.21	5.4	...
Tofu, 4% fat	1.9	7	42	...	0.06	0.03	0.1	...
Cow's milk, 3.7% fat	...	50	140	150	0.03	0.17	0.1	1
Soymilk, 1.5% fat	0.8	...	...	40	0.08	0.03	0.2	...
Cottage cheese, 4.2% fat	0.3	229	85	170	0.03	0.25	0.1	...
Okara, 1.5% fat	3.0	...	95	...	0.04	0.02	0.1	...
Eggs, 11.5% fat	2.3	122	129	1,180	0.11	0.30	0.1	...
Yogurt, 3.4% fat	...	47	132	140	0.03	0.16	...	0.1

The most readily available variety is Kanrich. Better are Japanese varieties bred especially for tofu making, and available either through some Asian food supply stores or directly from tofu producers. Such varieties can be expensive, so if the variety is not important to you, then plant beans bought in bulk from feed stores. You'll still get an excellent tofu. Later, once you are an experienced grower, you might prefer spending the extra money to grow varieties particularly bred for the curdling process.

Requiring about 100 days to mature, soybeans can be grown over a wide range. They like a soil suited to growing string beans, except that soybeans do best in slightly more alkaline conditions with a pH of 6 to 7. Soybeans thrive in a humus-enriched soil in which the phosphorus and potash content has been boosted by the addition of wood ash plus granite dust or other similar rock fertilizer.

Soybeans can take more cold than most other beans. A standard guideline is to plant when the apple trees in your area are in full bloom. If there aren't any apple trees around to use as an index of the season, plant after the last expected hard frost; the soil should be warmed so that the seed will not rot before it can germinate. Plant one inch deep, with plants to be thinned to seven or so inches apart in each direction, in beds rather than rows. The plants will thus form a bed of living mulch, keeping down weeds. Before planting, seed should be inoculated with a nitrogen-fixing bacteria, available at any nursery supply store. This further increases production.

Few insects bother soybeans, but rabbits like them better than almost anything. In fact, they are often planted as a lure to draw rabbits away from other crops (which shows how much this country has to learn about the value of soybeans). Rotate the planting of soybeans with crops that are not in the legume family (those that are not beans or peas) in order to discourage brown spot, bacterial blight, and downy mildew.

Soybeans are delicious eaten green, and the only way you are likely to even be able to have them that way is to grow some yourself. Pick when the pods are almost fully mature but before they begin to turn yellow. You can boil them briefly to make it easier to shell the beans. For dried beans and tofu making, allow to hang until dry on the vine, but no longer, or the pods may split, spilling the beans over the ground. The vines and empty pods are valuable additions to the soil as a green manure, and should be turned under.

Soybeans grow slowly at first, often allowing weeds to outgrow and overtake them. Weeds left in the plot can greatly reduce yields, and you'll likely need to keep them under control by shallow cultivation. You can give beans a head start by sprouting them prior to planting.

As for the actual yield of the crop, expect it to be about the same as peas and better than lima beans: a 100-foot row should yield about 30 pounds, half of which is pods.

Of course all of these growing suggestions are dependent upon your having ample area to devote to soybeans, and it's understandable if you're reluctant to give up precious garden space that could be planted in more expensive crops.

3 Making Tofu

Even if you can buy tofu locally, there are still several good reasons for making it yourself. Not only is making tofu economical, but it can be fun as well. You'll also get okara and whey, valuable foods you can't buy.

By making your own tofu, you know more about the quality of the food you are putting in your mouth. Homemade is fresher than store-bought; if tofu has yet to catch on big locally, it has likely been sitting around for days, losing flavor by the hour.

In many areas of the country, you have no choice—tofu is unavailable, or at best, a few cakes show up sporadically at a natural food store.

The equipment

You'll need a means of grinding the soaked soybeans. A blender is the best tool, but you can make do with a food mill or grinder—it's just a little more work.

Next you'll want a big pot, such as a canning kettle; it should be stainless steel or enameled, not aluminum. These are often available at hardware, variety and secondhand stores. You can also get them through mail-order houses, including Sears, Roebuck & Co. and

Montgomery Ward & Co. If you do any canning, you probably have just such a kettle already, and if you don't, you certainly should—they are one of the most useful things you could have in your kitchen. You'll find yourself using it for many things besides tofu making and canning.

You'll also use a colander at various stages of the process.

Another large pot or bowl, with a capacity of 1½ to 2 gallons, is needed to catch the soymilk as it is strained from the pressing sack.

Unfamiliar pieces of equipment you will need are a pressing sack, a settling cloth, and mold. The pressing sack can be made very easily. It should conform in shape to the colander or strainer you will be using. Sew the bag with the strongest stitch and thread you have. Use a French seam or stretch stitch or zigzag stitch to enable the bag to withstand a lot of strain.

For use with one-pound lots of dry soybeans and the standard colander, the best pressing sack is roughly triangular (or funnel shaped) with a top measurement of about 20 inches and a depth of about 14 inches. This allows you to open the sack fully over the top of the colander and provides enough depth to handle all of the mash from the batch in the recipe that follows. The sack should be rounded at the bottom.

The best materials for the pressing sack are unbleached muslin, gauze-type material, or several layers of cheesecloth. Synthetic curtain materials are very good because of their strength and because they are very easy to wash.

The settling cloth, used to line the mold, can be made from the same material and should be cut large enough to fold over the settling curds.

You will probably have to improvise a mold for separating the curds from the whey. Of several homemade versions the easiest is a colander; a small plate can be used for a lid. This produces tofu of a rather funny shape, but works well. A mold can be fashioned from a rectangular plastic container, perforated with ¼-inch holes. The holes can be made with a heated nail or knitting needle. A two-pound coffee can will also work, but the holes are more difficult to make. You must remove both ends and drill a series of ¼-inch holes in the sides, filing off burrs so that the cloths will slip out easily. Also place holes in the accompanying plastic lid. Save the metal lid for pressing. Replace the plastic lid on the can and line with the settling cloth. Tofu made in a can will be just the right shape to store inside a plastic bag in another coffee can.

Another simple mold is made from a 5 x 9-inch aluminum bread

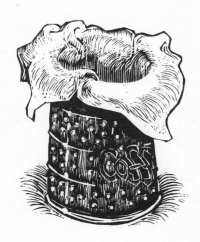

pan, drilled or punched over its sides and bottom. A perforated plastic refrigerator container will also serve.

For those who are handy, a mold can be fashioned from wood or high-fired ceramic stoneware. Stoneware won't absorb moisture, and therefore, stays clean.

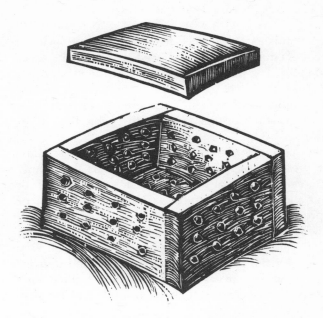

You can order a tofu kit, complete with wooden press, sack, cloth, and nigari, from The Learning Tree, P.O. Box 76, Bodega, CA 94922.

And then there are the usual odds and ends: measuring spoons and cups, stirring spoons, spatula, and other things you probably already have on hand.

The solidifier

Just as rennet is used to curdle milk in making dairy cheese, certain salts are used to obtain the same effect in making tofu. These agents actually draw out the soymilk protein and gather it together into curds, leaving the clear whey. The traditional agent is known as nigari, a pale pink salt from evaporated sea water. It is available by mail from The Learning Tree, mentioned above. Less expensive and easier to come by is Epsom salt (hydrated magnesium sulfate, $MgSO_47H_2O$). This salt is stocked by all drugstores, and five-pound bags are very inexpensive. Your drugstore may also be able to supply you with other solidifiers: calcium chloride, calcium sulfate (gypsum), or magnesium chloride. Despite their ominous names, all are naturally occurring minerals and pose no threat to your system when used in the minute quantities required in tofu making. In fact, they actually can be valuable supplements to the diet.

Soybean cheese can be at least as calcium-rich as dairy cheese if a calcium salt, such as calcium sulfate, is used. Tofu made with Epsom salt will have a generous magnesium content. We prefer to mix our solidifiers, in order to have both calcium and magnesium well represented in the tofu. Tailor the proportions of each to suit the needs of your own diet.

You can also use acetic acid or citric acid, in the form of vinegar and lemon juice, but these curdling agents contribute a taste and produce a granular texture that some find inferior. Experiment for yourself.

Table 4
Solidifers for tofu

	Amount added to 1 c. water for 1 qt. soymilk	Amount added to 3 c. water for 1 gal. soymilk
Magnesium sulfate (Epsom salt)	$1/3$–$1/2$ tsp.	$1^1/3$–2 tsp.
Calcium sulfate (gypsum)	$1/3$–$1/2$ tsp.	$1^1/3$–2 tsp.
Calcium chloride	$1/4$ tsp.	1 tsp.
Magnesium chloride	$1/4$ tsp.	1 tsp.
Nigari	$1/2$ tsp.	2 tsp.
Sea water	$1/3$–$1/2$ c.	1–$1^1/3$ c.
Vinegar or lemon juice (without dilution)	1 tsp.	4 tsp.

The process

STEP 1

You'll need:
     1 pound dry soybeans (approximately 2¼ cups)
     large bowl
     colander

Rinse the beans. Cover them with enough cold water to allow for expansion. Soak overnight.

Drain the beans and rinse again before using. If you can't make tofu by the next day, you can store the beans in a plastic bag in the refrigerator for up to a week or in the freezer for up to 3 months. On the other hand, don't try to hasten the soaking process by partially cooking the beans, either because you forgot to soak the beans the night before or just now decided you want tofu burgers tonight; this seems like an obvious solution, but it just doesn't work and is guaranteed to gum up your pressing sack.

STEP 2

You'll need:
    blender, meat grinder, or what have you
    water
    measuring cup
    large canning kettle

Blender method:
Apply a nonstick surface, such as oil or liquid lecithin, to the pot. Heat 2 cups water in the pot on low with a trivet or another device placed underneath to reduce the heat's intensity.

Blend beans, using 1½ cups water to 1 cup of soaked beans. Add batches to the pot as you blend.

The beans will have now expanded to about 7½ cups, so you will be using about 11 cups of water. Use another cup to rinse the blender into the cooking pot. Total water used up to this point will be about 14 cups.

Grinder method:
Grind the beans as fine as possible, perhaps using a medium and then a fine screen, grinding them twice. Begin with the same amount of water as above, 14 cups, and add the bean mash to the water.

The amount of water used is actually not critical. Excess water will simply be strained out into the whey after you have pressed the tofu; there is only a certain amount of soy solids in a given amount of beans, and adding too much water will not change that in the slightest. Using less water will mean harder work for your blender (beware of burned-out blenders!) but will not alter the resulting tofu appreciably. The thicker the mixture, the more likely a skin will form on top, as happens with boiling milk. (In Japan, this skin is considered a delicacy.)

The amount of water used should be tallied as you go, because it is easy to lose count.

STEP 3

Cook the soy mixture over a medium fire, loosely covered. Bring to a rolling boil, reduce heat, and simmer for at least 15 to 20 minutes.

The cooking time is important, as raw soybeans contain a factor known as the trypsin inhibitor. Essentially, this means that the protein contained in the beans cannot be properly assimilated by the body unless the beans are adequately cooked.

You have now used 14 or 15 cups of water, leaving 15 to go.

STEP 4

You'll need:
> pressing sack
> colander
> large pot

While the beans are cooking, prepare the pressing utensils. Wet the sack and place it in the colander, then place the colander over the pot.

It's best to place the pot in the sink, as the next step tends to be a bit sloppy. Also, you'll be working at a more comfortable level.

STEP 5

Pour the cooked mixture into the pressing sack to separate out the soymilk. Rinse the empty pot with 1 cup of water and pour the residue into the sack. Wash the cooking pot and apply a nonstick surface again. Transfer the strained soymilk to the large pot and place on the stove once more. Reserve 2 cups of water to mix with solidifier. Use the remaining 12 cups to cool the mixture so that it can be handled. Pour 4 cups at a time through the soy mixture; allow to drain. After the last of the water is added you can begin to press, squeeze, or twist to dry the pulp as much as possible. Add soymilk to that already on the stove as the pressing pot fills. Heat again to boiling.

At this point you will have made *soymilk*. You can stop here, cool the liquid, and use it as you would dairy milk. (See page 37 for information on fortifying soymilk.) Perhaps you'll want to save a quart or so and devote the rest to making tofu; if so, you must reduce the amount of solidifier used accordingly.

We use 3 teaspoons of solidifier to 30 cups of water, or 1 teaspoon to 10 cups. If you remove a ½ gallon of the milk (8 cups), use about 2⅛ teaspoons of solidifier salt instead of 3. (You can figure approximately ⅛ teaspoon of solidifier to 1 cup liquid.)

Store the residue, known as *okara,* in the container and refrigerate, or dry it as explained in Chapter 5. Read there of the many uses of this free food.

STEP 6

You'll need:
>   2 cups water
>   2 to 3 teaspoons solidifier salts

>   *or*

>   6 tablespoons vinegar or lemon juice

>   *or*

>   3 cups fresh, clean sea water

Dissolve the solidifier salts in water; when the soymilk returns to a boil, remove from the heat to add the solidifier. The soymilk must reach the boiling point if it is to curdle properly.

(As mentioned before, tofu can be made with vinegar or lemon juice, but these impart a flavor and granular texture. We prefer the various salts.)

STEP 7

You'll need:
>   measuring cup
>   wooden spoon

Add about ¾ cup solidifier solution and stir vigorously to distribute it evenly throughout the soymilk. Stop the movement in the milk by back-stirring and, when it becomes still, check to see if the curdling process has begun. If it has not, add another ¼ cup, stirring gently, and cover the pot.

After 5 minutes, examine again. If the soymilk has properly curdled, the whey will appear clear and yellowish. If it is still milky, add solidifier slowly until the curds definitely separate from the whey.

The manner in which the solidifier is added is not nearly so important as the amount. Too much solidifier can spoil the tofu, so it is best to be cautious and add as little as you can to achieve delicate, light curds.

If you add too much solidifier, the effect will be visible immediately. The curds will clump together in a tight mass and collect at the bottom of the pot. Don't despair—you can still use the tofu. It will be more solid and tougher, but you may even prefer it that way.

Experience is the best teacher. You will discover that the various solidifiers and combinations of solidifier will act differently. You may even find that certain varieties of bean produce a distinctive tofu.

STEP 8

You'll need:
   settling cloth
   tofu mold
   settling pan to catch the whey
   weight (a can or a stone of about a pound will do)

Moisten the settling cloth with water and line the mold. Place the mold over a large pan in the sink. Ladle as much of the clear whey as possible from the pan and pour it through the settling cloths to strain it. Ladle the curds gently into the mold. When all the curds are in the mold, fold the settling cloth over the curds, place the lid on the mold, and add the weight on top. Press the tofu for 20 minutes, or until the whey has stopped dripping from the mold.

The tofu may be either removed under cold water or left in the mold until cool, with the weight removed.

Store tofu under water in the refrigerator, and change the water at least every other day. It will be fresh for a week or more, but acquires a pink tinge around the edges in time. Revitalize older tofu by parboiling it.

Making tofu in quantity

Most people start off making tofu with about a pound of beans per batch, yielding 2½ pounds or so of the finished product—not very much for a family of tofu enthusiasts. The options are either to make tofu a few times a week, or to make a larger quantity. With 3½ pounds of beans you can make a family-size batch of 8 or 9 pounds.

Quantity tofu making requires some larger-scale equipment and a bit of help from the family.

You'll need:
    2 large pots, with covers, holding at least 5 gallons apiece
    large pressing sack
    large tofu mold (this can be used both for pressing the soy mash and for settling the tofu)
    large settling cloth
    some sort of mechanical press
    solidifier salts

1. Rinse thoroughly 3½ pounds of dry beans. Soak overnight, covering the beans with enough water to allow for expansion.

2. In the morning, heat 1½ gallons of water in a 5-gallon pot.

3. Grind the beans in a blender in the proportion of 1 cup of soaked beans to 1½ cups of water. You will have about 26 cups of soaked beans and will be adding about 40 cups (2½ gallons) of water. Add the beans to the heating water as you grind them.

If you have no electricity or no electrical appliances, grind the beans in a flour mill, in a meat grinder with a fine screen, or by whatever means you may have. Grind the soaked beans without adding water, pouring this water into the pot instead. Be sure to keep a tally of the water used, as it's easy to lose count.

4. Bring the contents of the pan to a boil, stirring frequently to minimize sticking. When the foam rises (or overflows, if you are not attentive), the mash is boiling. Lower the heat and simmer for at least 15 to 20 minutes to liberate the protein; it is important to cook the mixture well in order to undo the trypsin factor which interferes with protein digestion.

5. Moisten the pressing sack and arrange it in the settling box of the mechanical press. Ladle the hot mash into the sack, allowing the soymilk to drain off into a large pot placed below the press. Press and then add the remainder of the water to total 6½ gallons. Press again. You can, at this point, remove some of the soymilk and make tofu from the rest; if you are just making soymilk, this step completes the process.

6. Save the okara for refrigeration or drying. Return the soymilk to the stove and heat it to a boil.

7. Prepare the solidifier while waiting for the pot to boil. Use 4

cups of water to 3 tablespoons of solidifier salt. Or, measure 1¼ cups of freshly squeezed lemon juice or 1 cup vinegar without dilution.

8. When the mixture begins to boil, remove it from the heat, add about 1½ cups of solidifier, and stir briskly. Stop the agitation by back-stirring and examine the milk. If it has not begun to curdle, add another cup and stir gently. Cover and let stand for about 5 minutes. Examine the mixture again. The whey should be a clear yellow. If it is still milky, add solidifier and stir gently until the curds definitely separate from the whey.

9. Line the mold with the pressing cloth and place it over a large pot to collect the whey. Ladle the curds carefully into the mold, working slowly to allow whey to drain out. When all the curds are in the container, fold the cloth over the top of the curds, place the lid on top, and weight it down with an object weighing about 4 pounds. The curds may then be pressed gently under the mechanical press used for the mash. More weight will result in a firmer product, so experiment to find the density you like best. (Density is also determined by the amount of solidifier used: more will result in firmer tofu.)

10. Press for from 10 to 30 minutes, or until whey no longer drips from the settling mold.

11. Invert the form under cold water in a large pan or sink; allow the tofu to cool before removing the cloths. Or, if you prefer, the tofu can cool in the mold itself. Cut into convenient-size squares and refrigerate under water. Change the water every day or so. When properly refrigerated and stored under water, tofu will keep for at least a week.

4 Using Tofu

Before trying the recipes, let's become acquainted with the several personalities of tofu in its various forms.

Fresh tofu

Fresh tofu will keep for about a week when refrigerated under water in a closed container, such as a plastic box, glass or stainless steel bread pan (aluminum is not satisfactory), or plastic bag inside a coffee can. The water should be changed at least every other day to keep the tofu at its optimum freshness.

With each day that it is stored, tofu changes slightly, becoming denser and slightly stronger in flavor. It is at its most delicate when very fresh, and best suited then for recipes in which the subtle flavor of tofu is allowed to shine through. Use older tofu in recipes that derive their flavor from other ingredients.

In a short time you will become such a devotee that you can detect subtle variations in the flavor of fresh tofu. Tofu made from nigari is very light and delicate, as is tofu solidified with Epsom salt. Other solidifiers, such as calcium sulfate and magnesium chloride, will produce a denser curd with its own personality. You may prefer one to another; it is all a matter of personal taste.

Each batch you make will differ slightly (perhaps almost imperceptibly) from the one before it, just as your bread will differ from your neighbor's even though you both use the same recipe. It is a function of different amounts and techniques. Though one batch of tofu may be lighter than another, both will contain the same percentage of nutrients present in the soymilk. If you have either accidentally or intentionally used more solidifier than is necessary, the tofu will be very dense. The process may be less efficient than usual, but the nutritional content should be about the same. The difference is only in the water content.

How to revive aging tofu

Tofu can be restored to freshness by parboiling. Cut the tofu in two-inch cubes and place them in a pot with enough cold water to cover. Bring to a boil, reduce the heat, and simmer for about four minutes. Allow the boiled tofu to drain on a clean towel. More cooking will make the tofu tougher in texture, but this could be just the consistency you want for a particular recipe or effect; the texture works well in recipes where it replaces meat, and you might want to parboil fresh tofu to obtain a firmer texture for some uses.

Making firmer tofu

If firmer tofu is required for a recipe, you can press out some of the water by placing the block on an inclined board or dish, weighting it, and allowing the water to run off.

Wrap the tofu in cheesecloth, a clean dish towel, or paper towels to maintain its form. Place a plate or board on top and weight it down with a heavy can or a convenient rock. The water can be removed very quickly by wrapping the tofu in a clean towel or in the pressing sack used for tofu making, and then twisting. This will deform the tofu, so it is a technique best used when you don't need tofu's square shape for a recipe.

Freezing it

You should never have to throw tofu away. If you have more than you can use, freeze it. First drain it and place it in a plastic bag. Be sure to expel all of the air from the bag, tie it securely, and freeze immediately. When you've collected several bags, you can make a batch of PSP—processed soy protein. You may have encountered this product, known by the trademark TVP, as an ingredient in many commercially prepared foods and economy hamburger blends. Your own homemade processed soy protein will be fresher and even more meatlike, if that is your desire, than the commercial product. Learn to make it in Chapter 7.

Serving it plain and simple

Does a true connoisseur of tofu really need a book of recipes to make the food more interesting? Well, at first you will, but given time to get acquainted, you'll enjoy tofu straight. If you make your own, you'll be treated to tofu at its best—warm, and right out of the mold. It is as appealing as freshly baked bread.

Plain tofu is marvelous for dipping. If you want to be traditional about it, serve chilled bite-size cubes in a lotus bowl, accompanied by sauces and garnishes. You might try soy sauce (tamari), Mustard Sauce, tahini, either commercial or homemade, Shrimp Sauce, Wine and Garlic Sauce, Walnut Sauce, Miso Sauce (all on pages 135), or your own creation. Tofu slices are a fine addition to sandwiches of all types. Tofu will earn its place, and its own initial, in the traditional BLT. It adds interest and moisture to all types of garden sandwiches, replacing mayonnaise or avocado for the diet-conscious. Served on whole grain bread, tofu makes a high-protein sandwich in which meat would be entirely redundant.

Cubed tofu goes well in all kinds of soups, especially in our Minestrone (page 96) and Ukranian Borscht (page 97). The fresh curds, removed from the tofu-making pot before pressing, are delightful additions to clear broths, where they have the appearance of tiny clouds floating in a soup sky.

Try putting cubed tofu in all of your favorite tossed salads; it will contribute protein and a new texture.

As you add to your knowledge of tofu and its many personalities, you will undoubtedly find your own ways to add to this primer of uses—and we certainly encourage you to do just that, for the manifold uses of this amazing food have yet to be exploited.

Tofu for vegetarians

There are several grades of vegetarianism, with varying degrees of restrictions. Most vegetarians eschew red meat, poultry, and likely, seafood as well. Total vegetarians, or vegans, also rule out eggs and dairy products. Tofu can offer great variety to such diets, but many vegetarian cookbooks oddly give only a cursory nod to this food. We offer dozens of recipes for the milk-and-eggs vegetarian. Making nutritional ends meet for the vegan is more demanding, however, and while tofu and its by-products can be an important part of such a diet, we don't feel qualified to discuss the requirements of a vegan diet. Readers should refer to *The Vegetarian Alternative* by Vic Sussman (Emmaus, Pa.: Rodale Press, 1978) and *Laurel's Kitchen: A Handbook for Vegetarian Cookery & Nutrition* by Laurel Robertson, Carol Flinders, and Bronwen Godfrey (Petaluma, Calif.: Nilgiri Press, 1977). A number of our recipes involve no animal ingredients whatsoever.

Tofu for dieters

A nice thing about tofu is that you can eat a lot of a tofu dish without being swamped in calories. While this makes eating more fun for all of us, perennial dieters benefit the most. No longer do they have to put up with doll-size portions or kinky all-meat or citrus fruit regimens. A tofu-based meal can offer a satisfying volume of food. And tofu offers plenty of protein without excessive calories, as few foods can.

It's vital to keep at or just above the recommended protein level for good health; eat too little, and the body will borrow that all-important commodity from itself. The accompanying table (table 5) suggests the optimum daily protein intake for healthy men and women. It does not take into consideration that people suffering from psychological or physical trauma, such as caused by injury or surgery, temporarily will need more protein. Note that a pregnant or lactating woman's needs are greater.

For the dieter, the calorie and protein figures are critical. The protein figure is to be heeded closely, while the calorie figure is the variable: cut calories, but see to it that protein is not sacrificed.

When we started experimenting with tofu as an egg substitute, things went so well at first that we soon had high hopes of it fitting every recipe calling for eggs. But we had a few disappointments. For one, tofu does not make custards or light cheese soufflés. It does, however, do well in emulsified sauces, in semi-soufflés, and with vegetables and legumes. These recipes include Tofu Mayonnaise (page 105), Tofu Hollandaise Sauce (page 131), Tofu Bearnaise Sauce (page 132), Creamy Tofu Mustard Sauce (page 133), and Persian Pancakes (page 143).

If the egg habit is tough to break but you would still like to reduce that early morning dose of cholesterol, try cutting the eggs with tofu.

Table 5

Recommended daily calorie and protein allowances

	Age (yrs.)	Weight (lbs.)	Height (in.)	Calories	Protein (gr.)
Children	1–3	28	34	1,300	23
	4–6	44	44	1,800	30
	7–10	66	54	2,400	36
Males	11–14	97	63	2,800	44
	15–18	134	69	3,000	54
	19–22	147	69	3,000	54
	23–50	154	69	2,700	56
	51+	154	69	2,400	56
Females	11–14	97	62	2,400	44
	15–18	119	65	2,100	48
	19–22	128	65	2,100	46
	23–50	128	65	2,000	46
	51+	128	65	1,800	46
Pregnant				+300	+30
Lactating				+500	+20

You can even scramble straight tofu, but the results aren't quite as egglike.

Becoming an innovator

A book of soyfood recipes can't come close to exploring all the possibilities inherent in tofu, okara, whey, and soymilk. The following suggestions should help you develop your own cuisine.

Tofu can be used:

1. as a main protein source in casseroles and one-dish meals of all kinds;
2. as a meat substitute in most all ground-beef recipes, either in its original form or as PSP (processed soy protein);
3. in meat dishes, replacing some or most of the meat;
4. as a cheese replacement in dishes calling for cottage cheese, ricotta, or cream cheese;
5. as a mayonnaise substitute;

Table 6
To suggest how tofu can be used in high-volume, low-calorie, high-protein menus, here is a sample day's meals.

Breakfast	Calories	Protein in Grams
2 medium scrambled eggs	156	15
1 slice whole grain bread	62	2
½ c. skimmed milk yogurt	61	4
¼ c. bran cereal	35	2
	314	23

Lunch		
1 Tia's Tofu Sandwich with 1 slice whole wheat bread	132	10
8 oz. fortified skimmed milk	105	10
	237	20

Dinner		
2 tbsp. any dip with vegetables	58	3.8
3½ × 3½-in. square of Eggplant Casserole Italienne	239	12.7
1 c. brown rice	178	3.8
⅔ c. coleslaw with dressing	68	2.3
⅓ c. Spanish Creme dessert	93	4.8
	636	27.4
Totals for day	1,187 cal.	70.4 gr.

6. to reduce cholesterol in egg-based dishes, using half the eggs called for;
7. in place of (or in addition to) sour cream and yogurt in dips and dressings;
8. as an egg replacement in quick breads;
9. instead of eggs in waffles and pancakes;
10. in place of eggs as a stabilizer and emulsifier in sauces and salad dressings;
11. instead of or in addition to eggs in soufflés;
12. in eggless allergy cooking;

27

13. in scrambled eggs;
14. instead of eggs and cream in rich desserts.

Okara can be used:

1. in baked goods (except the most delicate of cakes) to add lightness and texture;
2. as a high-fiber addition to hot cereals, casseroles, patties, meat loaves, and soufflés;
3. in pancakes, waffles, and crepes;
4. as a filler in low-calorie diet foods;
5. in pastries, pie crusts, yeast doughs, and quick breads;
6. in poultry stuffings;
7. in soft cookies (wet okara) and crisp ones (dry okara);
8. in pet food.

Whey can be used:

1. as a base for soups;
2. as cooking water for vegetables;
3. as a base for sauces, stews, and gravies;
4. instead of milk in yeast doughs;
5. in pet foods;
6. as a mild, safe soap;
7. to water plants.

Soymilk can be used:

1. in all cooking calling for milk;
2. in allergy diets;
3. in baby food and as a milk for children;
4. as milk for strict vegetarians (vegans).

Okara
and Whey 5

Make your own tofu, and you end up with both a clear whey and fibrous leavings, somewhat like mashed potatoes in consistency, called okara.

Okara

If you make tofu or soymilk even occasionally, you are going to end up with a lot of okara, so it's good to know some delicious and practical ways to use it. This innocuous-looking food, seemingly without potential or character, deserves consideration.

One nice thing about okara is that it will add fiber to your diet. A lack of fiber, as almost everyone knows, can lead to internal disorders. Fruits, vegetables, legumes, and whole grain flours are good sources of fiber. But you can also increase your fiber intake by adding it to the family's favorite dishes. Bran is often used for this purpose. Bran itself is a highly nutritious by-product of milling flour; the outer parts of the wheat grains are stripped away in order to produce white (refined) flour. Whole grain flour retains this bran; but the typical American diet still lacks sufficient roughage.

Bran is normally accepted as the standard when it comes to bulk in a diet, and, in addition, it is usually considered to be the most inexpensive source of such fiber. Consider okara, which rivals bran as a source of nutrition and fiber. It is available for free if you make your own tofu, while unprocessed bran is difficult to find outside of a natural foods store. Many people who supplement their diets with bran do so in its commercially prepared and often sugar-laden form; okara is free of additives. Okara is also much lower in calories and higher in protein (it contains about 17 percent of the soybean's protein content).

Perhaps the easiest way to use okara at first is as a meat extender in meat loaf, hamburger patties, homemade sausage, and the like. (Substituting okara for meat is covered more thoroughly in the various recipes.) The okara reduces the cost of the meal by replacing some meat; it thereby also lowers cholesterol intake and, of course, adds fiber.

Okara can be used with seafood and poultry. The flavor comes right through. Try it in casseroles, chowders (where it increases bulk while not altering the flavor), croquettes, loaves, and stuffings.

Okara may be at its best used to enhance baked goods, holding moisture to keep things fresh longer than you would expect: biscuits, coffee cakes, quick loaves, muffins, pancakes, waffles, pastries, and yeast breads will all benefit.

Okara can be added to soups to make them heartier and higher in protein. (It's not suited to clear soups, as it tends to cloud them.) Try adding ⅛ to ¼ cup per serving at first.

OKARA WITH OATMEAL

As scratchy as it looks when dry, oatmeal doesn't provide much fiber. Try supplementing it with okara, half and half. You'll still get the good oatmeal flavor. Here's how the two compare.

	One cup, wet (236 gr.)	
	Okara	Oatmeal
Fiber	5.42	0.5
Calories	156	148
Carbohydrate (gr.)	16	26
Protein (gr.)	8.3	5.4

In many recipes requiring leavening, eggs may be omitted if the necessary amount of leavening is increased by one teaspoon for each egg excluded. This works well in various hot and sweet breads; banana breads, zucchini breads, applesauce cakes, and the like have all turned out well, as have pancakes and waffles. Sometimes okara is used instead of egg, producing a light and moist result, and you can do some of your own experimenting. (We have had little luck replacing eggs in this manner with light, delicate cakes.)

The following recipes for baked foods use okara, sometimes with tofu, as a replacement for eggs: Batter for Deep Frying (page 87), Banana–Coconut–Tofu Bread (Eggless) (page 120), Okara Bran Biscuits (page 123), and Okara Tofu Spice Bars (Eggless) (page 158).

It is not possible to totally substitute soy products for wheat flour, but much flour can be replaced with okara without changing the ratios of the other ingredients. In some cases, when the okara is particularly wet, it is even necessary to add a bit more flour to take up that increased moisture.

Okara increases the fiber and protein content of baked goods, and enhances moisture and texture as well.

Dried okara is used in crisp cookies and almost everywhere you would use bread crumbs or cracker crumbs. It's well suited to baked dessert recipes, such as rice and bread puddings, and is a logical granola ingredient.

To dry okara, spread it shallowly on a cookie sheet in a very slow oven (250° to 275°F), above a radiator or pilot light, in a dehydrator, or under the sun. Stir from time to time to break up clumps. Okara is properly dried when it feels dry and crumbly to the touch. The color should be the same as when wet. Make the consistency smoother by powdering it by hand or fluffing it briefly in the blender.

Moist okara can be stored in the refrigerator, covered, for a week or more, but it will gradually spoil. Dried okara, on the other hand, will keep indefinitely. Two cups of wet okara weigh 14¼ ounces, diminishing to only 3½ ounces when dried.

Whey

Whey is the other by-product of tofu making. Like okara, it should be regarded as a food source rather than waste. Containing 9 percent of the protein of the original soybean, the whey from one pound of dry beans has a considerable 14 grams of protein. In addition, it has most of the water-soluble B vitamins and about 44 grams of sugars.

Whey is excellent as a base for soups, stews, sauces, and gravies. Many of the recipes throughout the book benefit from the use of whey in place of water. We've found that, used instead of water or milk in yeast breads, whey hastens the activity of the yeast.

Use whey instead of water when cooking vegetables. Its natural sweetness accents the flavor of the vegetables and makes it possible to use far less salt. This water, in turn, will pick up more valuable nutrients from the vegetables, making it a superb soup stock.

Before discarding any whey, try using it as a mild cleansing agent to wash up your tofu equipment and settling cloths.

If you have exhausted all of the above possibilities and still have whey on hand, moisten pet food with it or just sprinkle it over your garden. The nitrogen content and vitamins and minerals make it a valuable supplement for all kinds of living things.

And now to test the claims we've made for okara and whey, try any of the bread, pastry, and pancake and waffle recipes in this book; give whey a chance as soup stock in our recipes or your own.

A few of our favorite okara recipes follow immediately. Others include Garbanzo Okara Loaf (page 55), Tamale Pie (page 68), Okara Meat Croquettes (page 69), Okara Stuffing for Poultry (page 86), Okara Fry-and-Bake Coating (page 87), Sweet Pie Shell (page 152), and Fudge Brownies (page 156).

If you're caught short of okara, or if you buy your tofu and never have it on hand, then try substituting bread crumbs or bran for dry okara in many of these recipes.

Okara Patties

2 eggs
¼ to ½ cup oil
½ cup whole wheat flour
1 tablespoon cornstarch
(salt—optional)
pepper, to taste
1½ cups okara
nutmeg, to taste
ground cloves, to taste
½ cup onion, chopped
1 cup mixed raw or cooked
   vegetables, chopped
oil, for sautéing

These delectable patties should be grilled slowly and for a long time so that they become very crisp and evenly browned. Okara has a wonderful texture when prepared in this way.

While beating the eggs, add the oil slowly. Add the flour and cornstarch to make a batter, and beat well. Stir in salt and pepper.

Stir the okara into the batter. Add nutmeg and cloves in small amounts.

Sauté the onion and mixed vegetables in a small amount of oil, and mix into the batter. If the batter is too thick, thin slightly with whey or soymilk; if it is too thin, add some wheat germ. Let the mixture stand for at least 1 hour.

Form into cakes and fry or grill until crisp and golden brown.

Serve with green or yellow vegetables, and brown rice. A nice

change from rice is ala (wheat berries cooked as rice is). Try a sauce or gravy.
Yield: 8 to 10 patties

Banana Okara Bread

This easily made bread can double as a dessert.
Preheat oven to 350°F.

Cream together milk, banana, egg, butter, honey, and okara. Mix dry ingredients in a separate bowl and then add to banana mixture. Blend well, but do not beat. Add raisins and nuts if desired.

Pour the batter into a greased 5 x 9-inch pan. Bake at 350°F for about an hour.
Yield: 1 loaf

¼ cup soymilk or dairy milk
3 bananas, mashed
1 egg
½ cup butter or margarine
½ cup honey
½ cup okara
1 teaspoon baking powder
1 teaspoon baking soda
(salt—optional)
1½ cups whole wheat flour
¼ cup wheat germ
(½ cup chopped nuts—optional)
(½ cup raisins—optional)

Okara Oatmeal Hot Cereal

This excellent breakfast cereal supplies fiber and lowers calories without sacrificing good oatmeal flavor and texture. The cooking time can vary from just a few minutes to all night—some people like to cook hot cereals on the back burner or on the back of the wood stove for hours, while others want them in an instant.

Mix all ingredients and bring to a boil while stirring constantly. Cover the pan, reduce the temperature to very low, and cook until the cereal has reached the consistency you like.

Serve this cereal on a flat dish with a large pat of butter right in the middle. It is not necessary to add more milk because the milk is in the cereal, but that is a matter of taste, as is a topping of preserves or honey or cinnamon.
Yield: 4 servings

½ cup dry rolled oats
(salt—optional)
½ cup okara
¼ cup dry skimmed milk powder and 2½ cups water
or
1¼ cups soymilk or dairy milk and 1¼ cups water

Granola

3 cups rolled oats
1 cup dry okara
½ cup wheat germ
½ cup unprocessed bran
½ cup sesame seeds
1 cup coconut
½ cup chopped nuts,
    except peanuts
½ cup sunflower seeds
½ to 1 cup raisins
(cinnamon to
    taste—optional)
⅔ cup water
⅔ cup oil
⅔ cup honey

Variations
    Add the following to the
granola after baking, as
you please:
  • ½ cup dried apples
  • ½ cup chopped dates
      that have been rolled
      in whole wheat flour
  • ½ cup dried bananas
  • ½ cup other dried
      fruit

Mix dry ingredients together in a large bowl. Set aside.
    In a saucepan, mix water, oil, and honey and heat just enough to blend.
    Pour the honey mixture over the dry ingredients and mix well. Spread out thinly on 3 cookie sheets and bake in a slow (300°F) oven for 15 or 20 minutes, turning frequently until dry.
Yield: 10 cups

Soymilk 6

Soymilk doesn't taste like dairy milk, and we won't waste any words trying to make you think otherwise. Soymilk has its very own flavor, which you may or may not find satisfying. The characteristic beany taste can be avoided by preparing soymilk through a method developed by Cornell University, Ithaca, New York, given below. Our standard soymilk recipe involves nothing more than going halfway in making tofu—you stop short of stirring in the solidifier.

Making soymilk, therefore, is easier than making tofu. But should you prefer to buy commercial soymilk, keep an eye out for sweeteners and additives. You'll find that the flavor isn't up to that of homemade, and you can't beat the price of from 9 cents to 25 cents per gallon.

Soymilk is nearly as high in protein as dairy milk, while containing less carbohydrates and fat and no cholesterol. If soymilk is to be used as a dairy milk substitute, however, you should consider adding vitamin B_{12} and calcium. The fat and carbohydrate levels can also be brought up to those of dairy milk by adding oil and honey.

As is true of soybeans in any form, soymilk must be heated in order to undo the factor which prohibits the body from making use of the beans' protein. Simmering the milk for at least 10 to 15 minutes will accomplish this.

Soymilk recipes in this book

Try substituting soymilk for cow's milk, cup for cup, in your favorite recipes. To get you started, this chapter offers a couple of recipes that make good use of soymilk. Soymilk also is used in these recipes:

Cheese Rarebit (page 51), Tofu–Blue Cheese Dressing (page 107), Curry Sauce (page 134), Klondike Pancakes (page 141), Okara Whole Wheat Waffles (page 144), Rice Flour–Okara Waffles (page 145), French Toast (page 147), Risengrød (page 147), Basic Mousse (page 155), and Soy Shake (page 166).

How to make it
Soymilk 1

1 pound soybeans
1½ cups water to each cup of soaked beans plus 2 cups of water for the pot
1 cup water for rinsing blender

This is the same process we use on the way to making tofu, stopping after pressing the soymilk. If you are making soymilk only, this recipe will yield about 1½ gallons, and unless you have a large and growing family, that's a lot of milk. Soymilk has about the same refrigerator life as cow's milk; it will sour and spoil even under the best of conditions, so don't make more than you'll need for a few days' use—unless, perhaps, you do a lot of baking. We often draw off only a quart or two of milk and curdle the rest into tofu.

Wash the beans. Cover them with enough cold water to allow for expansion, and soak overnight.

The following day, heat 2 cups of water in a large pot. Meanwhile, blend the soaked beans (which will have expanded to about 7½ cups) at high speed in batches of 1 part beans to 1½ parts water. This should take about 2 minutes. Pour each batch into the cooking pot as you go.

The total water used to this point should be about 13¼ cups.

When the soy mixture comes to a boil, reduce the heat and maintain a simmer for 12 to 25 minutes.

Pour the cooked bean mash into the pressing sack that's placed in a colander over a pot. (The best spot for this operation is the sink, in case of spills.) Add cold water to encourage more milk to drain—use 3 cups of water for each cup of beans. That would be a total of 22½ cups, or 9¼ more cups.

The Cornell University process calls for fortifying the soymilk to bring it to the standard of cow's milk in both carbohydrate and fat content. The problem with the additives mentioned, oil and honey, is that honey makes the milk too sweet for some tastes, and the oil separates out. You really don't have to add the fat and sweetener; in fact, we feel that the milk is better without it. We do suggest you either add the B_{12} and calcium, or make very sure you receive these essential nutrients from other foods. B_{12}, which is found in adequate amounts only in animal products, can be added to each batch as a crushed pill; 25-I.U., 50-I.U., and 100-I.U. potencies are available in drug stores and natural food stores.

A word of caution about adding calcium: calcium lactate, one of the most common forms in which calcium is found, acts as a solidifier, and if you add this injudiciously to warm soymilk you may end up with a batch of poor tofu curds.

An alternative is calcium carbonate, also available in drugstores. Unlike calcium lactate, it is insoluble, and the soymilk must be stirred up well before each use to disperse this mineral throughout.

Soymilk made by the following Cornell University method yields fine tofu, with a flavor and texture that is unparalleled; we recommend the method as long as you don't mind juggling the boiling water involved.

Unless you use soymilk often, freeze whatever you won't need within a week. Thaw frozen soymilk in the refrigerator. If it should separate or have a strange texture, as cow's milk may under similar conditions, it can be restored by a minute in the blender.

300 milligrams calcium, from calcium lactate or calcium carbonate, for each cup of milk

50 to 150 micrograms vitamin B_{12} for the batch (of special importance to those eating no dairy products or meat)

1 teaspoon honey, for each cup of milk

1 teaspoon oil, for each cup of milk

Soymilk 2 (The Cornell University Process)

One of the major objections to soymilk is a strong taste that is caused by lipoxidase, an enzyme released when the beans are ground in cool water. Cornell University developed a method of eliminating the strong flavor by using boiling water as a grinding medium. This presents some problems, not the least of which is the danger of getting burned. (Work on the counter next to the stove so that all the hot containers will be close to one another.)

Precautions must be taken to prevent blender jars from breaking; plastic blender jars craze from the heat and won't last long. The best

1 pound soybeans
4 quarts boiling water
large pot
slotted spoon
measuring cups

jar for this process is one of stainless steel, but a glass jar is adequate if you are careful to preheat it with boiling water.

Wash the beans. Cover them with enough water to allow for expansion and soak overnight. Rinse them again in the morning, place in a bowl (metal preferably), and cover with some of the boiling water. This will preheat the beans.

Warm the blender jar by rinsing it first with very hot water and then boiling water.

Remove beans to a measuring cup with a slotted spoon and put them in the blender, 1 cup to 1½ cups boiling water. Wrap a folded dish towel around the jar to help prevent burns. (To prevent splashing, start the blender with the beans alone and add the water gradually, increasing the speed as you go.)

Cook the mash until it reaches a boil again and reduce the heat to maintain a simmer for about 30 minutes.

Pour the cooked bean mash through the pressing sack and add cold water to total 22½ cups for the entire amount.

(At this point you may draw off the milk you want and go on to make tofu, adding more water to bring the proportion to 4:1.)

Fortify as for Soymilk 1, then refrigerate immediately.
Yield: 5½ quarts

Koumiss

Koumiss is a fermented milk, a close relative of yogurt. It originated with the Arabs and other Middle Eastern peoples, and was originally made from mare's milk. Our soymilk koumiss saves you the trouble of milking mares.

Fermented milks are special for the healthful properties they pick up when undergoing fermentation. The B vitamins are increased, and the beneficial bacteria are an aid to the digestive tract. In addition, the bubbles are fun.

This thick, creamy beverage is very effervescent and slightly alcoholic. It should be made in a heavy champagne bottle for safety's sake. The pressure that builds up also demands that the bottle be stopped well; the most secure method is to drive in a cork and top that with a standard bottle cap. Caps and cappers are available at hardware stores and wine supply shops.

There's no need to stash this beverage in the basement for aging—it's ready to drink in a day or so. We serve it by uncapping it, mixing it briefly with fruit and sweetener in the blender, and pouring it into stemmed glasses. Don't try adding fruit or extra sweetener to the soymilk that goes into the bottle—the yeast would have a field day, turning the sugars into alcohol and producing enough carbon dioxide to make trouble in the form of a koumiss geyser or flying glass.

Soy Koumiss

Stir the yeast and honey into the warm water. Warm the soymilk to about 75°F, and stir in the above mixture. Pour immediately into a champagne bottle, and seal with a tight-fitting cork, bottle cap, or both. The cork should be wired in place if not capped.

Lay the bottle on its side for 5 hours or so at room temperature. Then refrigerate the bottle on its side for 20 to 24 hours, turning it from time to time.

Be careful when you open the bottle—it's going to pop, just like champagne.

Koumiss has an odd but delightful flavor, and is at its best mixed in the blender for a few seconds with pureed fruit. Try banana, peach, apricot, strawberry, pineapple, cherry, or whatever comes to mind. Other flavorings include honey, coconut, vanilla, or carob.

⅛ teaspoon dry yeast
2 teaspoons honey
2 tablespoons warm water
2 cups soymilk

Milkshakes

An obvious role for soymilk is in milkshakes. Kids will drink glass after glass, instead of soda and other sugary drinks.

To each blenderful, you can add 2 teaspoons calcium lactate, calcium gluconate, or bone meal powder to boost the calcium content to the equivalent of cow's milk. As for the flavoring ingredients, they are up to you. We all have different preferences, so make up your own recipes.

The following recipe for a peach milkshake can be considered a prototype. Frozen fruits will also work, but you may have to use less honey if the fruits have been frozen with added sugar.

Peach Milkshake

Place ingredients in a blender jar and blend well. Serve chilled.

2 medium-size peaches
1 teaspoon vanilla extract
¼ cup honey
1½ cups soymilk

Carob Shake Concentrate

½ cup honey
½ cup carob powder
¼ cup cold water

Mix these ingredients and bring them to a boil over slow heat. This syrup may be stored and used in a shake by adding 2 tablespoons syrup to 1 cup of soymilk.

Processed
Soy
Protein (PSP) 7

Textured Vegetable Protein (TVP) is the well-known trademarked name of a commercial soy product used to simulate meat, fish, poultry, and cured meats. It is made by extrusion from soy flour and can be purchased in many grocery stores and most natural food stores. It comes in a granular form, is generally brown in color, and is flavored to resemble beef. Economy hamburger mixes often contain soy in this form. Textured soy protein is also a main ingredient of most commercial mock-meats for vegetarians.

What is Processed Soy Protein?

We are going to introduce you to a processed soy protein you can make yourself from tofu. We'll call it PSP. You should find it better than the commercial product—fresher and even meatier.

PSP is an excellent use for leftover tofu. Perhaps your stored tofu is not as fresh as you would like it to be; maybe it has even turned pink around the edges and smells a little suspicious. It can be restored by simmering in water for 10 to 15 minutes.

Making PSP is very simple. You place the tofu in a plastic bag, expel as much of the air as possible, secure the bag, and wrap in freezer paper or a brown paper bag. Write the date on the package;

tofu can be left in the freezer up to three months.

When you are ready to make PSP, remove the frozen tofu from the freezer, unwrap, and place in a colander to thaw and drain. The product that you have after freezing will vary considerably, depending upon the original tofu. It may be honeycombed and brownish, or pale and much like the cakes from which it was made. It makes no difference—the results will be much the same.

After the tofu is thawed, press out as much water as possible: place it in a colander, sieve, or settling box for making tofu, wrap it with a clean towel or paper towels, and weight it down for 15 to 30 minutes. Or, simply put the tofu in a muslin dish towel or several layers of cheesecloth and twist the cloth around the tofu to press out the water.

After pressing, put the tofu in a large bowl and mash it with a fork, pastry blender, or potato masher, and then mix in flavoring as you please. To one cup pressed, thawed tofu, add any one of the following:

- 2 teaspoons soy sauce with garlic or onion powder, to taste
- 1 beef bouillon cube dissolved in the smallest possible amount of hot water
- 1 chicken bouillon cube, as above
- ¼ cup clam juice

Stir and mash the tofu until the flavoring is evenly distributed. The result is a wet PSP that can be either used as is or dried and stored for future use. The wet PSP must be stored in the refrigerator and should be used within a week, but the dry can be stored on the shelf and will keep indefinitely.

The wet product can be dried in a very slow (250° to 275°F) oven, toaster oven, solar dryer, or above a radiator or wood stove. Any warm place will do. Avoid scorching PSP as this absolutely destroys the flavor. When dry, store it in a closed container.

The recipes that follow are for either wet PSP or rehydrated dry PSP. The two differ in texture, and you may prefer one to the other. The wet is chewy and pleasant; the dry, when rehydrated, is almost impossible to tell from ground beef.

Reconstitute dry PSP by mixing it cup for cup with very warm water or whey. Stir and let stand for 15 minutes. If all the water is absorbed, the PSP will be of the proper consistency; if there is water left over, add it right along with the PSP in your recipe to maintain the proper bulk.

PSP recipes in this book

Add PSP to any ground meat dish to get away with less meat, less fat, and less cholesterol. You'll save money, too. Try our PSP recipes following page 73, as well as PSP Snack (page 86) and Clam Chowder with PSP (page 99).

The Recipes

Salt is optional or missing in most of the recipes in this book. The body's need for salt is ordinarily met by the natural sodium content of foods. By salting food in cooking and again at the table, you are adding more salt than your body needs, with a risk to health. Stop and think before you salt.

Main Dishes 8

Tofu, okara, and our Processed Soy Protein (PSP) find dozens of everyday applications in the recipes that follow. Here are casseroles, quiches, loafs, soufflés, and variations of international standards.

Main Dishes
Tofu Lasagna 47
Baked Stuffed Zucchini 47
Broiled Tofu Slices 48
Deep-Fried Sesame Tofu 49
Ravioli 50
Cheese Rarebit 51
Tofu Broccoli Casserole 51
Eggplant Casserole Italienne 52
Potato–Tofu–Cabbage Casserole 53
Tuna Tofu Casserole 53
Tofu Artichoke Casserole with Chicken or Tuna 54
Tortilla Casserole 55
Garbanzo Okara Loaf 55
Tofu Meat Loaf 56
Carrot Tofu Loaf 56

Carrots Parmesan with Tofu 57
Meatless Chili 57
Hot Tofu Tuna Salad 58
Corn and Tofu Soufflé 59
Spinach Soufflé 60
Vegetable Soufflé 60
Okara Zucchini Soufflé 61
Zucchini Entrée Squares 61
Lentil Stew 62
Kima (Indian Curry) 62
Tofu Enchiladas 63
Enchilada Sauce 63
Mushrooms à la Crème Tofu 64
Shrimp and Tofu 65
Okara–Mushroom–Shrimp Curry Patties 66
Tofu à la Newburg 66
Tofu Noodles Romanov 67
Almond–Vegetable–Tofu Sauté 67
Dow-Foo Chow Yoke (Stir-Fried Tofu) 68
Tamale Pie 68
Okara Meat Croquettes 69
Tofu Quiche 70
Vegetable Quiche 71
Pie Shell for Quiche 71
Green Peppers Stuffed with Tofu 72
Using Homemade PSP 73
Dinner Loaf with PSP 74
PSP Sloppy Joes 74
Stuffed Cabbage Rolls 75
Tacos 76
Carrot Tofu Loaf with PSP 76
Chili Con PSP 77
Spaghetti Sauce 78
PSP Stroganoff 78
Japanese-Style Meatballs 79
PSP Burgers 79
Skillet Supper 80
Stuffed Grape Leaves (Dolmadakia) 80
Pizza Dough with Okara 82
Pizza Sauce 82

Tofu Lasagna √√

Tofu lends itself beautifully to all sorts of ethnic foods, and is at its best in lasagna. This recipe makes a dish that tastes as if you used ricotta, but is much lighter than the standard lasagna.

(An interesting variation incorporates two layers of slightly cooked spinach, chopped and drained well.)

Cook the lasagna noodles, then douse with cold water and set aside. Have sauce, grated cheese, mushrooms, and parsley ready for assembly.

Mix tofu, Parmesan cheese, and garlic. Line the bottom of an oiled 8½ x 11-inch pan with a layer of noodles. Save those noodles in the best shape for the top layer. Sprinkle with about half of the mashed tofu mixture, half of the mushrooms, half of the parsley, about ½ cup of the sauce, and some of the cheese.

Now add another layer of noodles, and repeat the procedure with each of the fillings. Place the best noodles on top, sprinkle with the remaining grated cheese and top with the remaining tomato sauce.

Bake at 350°F for about 45 minutes or until nicely brown and blended throughout.

1 package whole wheat lasagna noodles
2 to 2½ cups spaghetti sauce
2 cups (½ pound) mozzarella, Swiss, or Monterey Jack cheese, grated
½ pound sautéed mushrooms
¼ cup parsley, chopped
1 cup tofu, mashed (or tofu slices for a layer effect)
¼ cup grated Parmesan cheese
crushed garlic or garlic powder to taste

Baked Stuffed Zucchini

Place the zucchini whole in a covered pot half-filled with water. Turn to boil for 2 minutes on each side. Remove from the water and cool.

Cook the rice until just done—still a bit chewy—and set aside.

Melt the butter over low heat. Add the onions and sauté until they become slightly transparent. Add the parsley and chopped mushrooms and sauté 1 minute longer, stirring constantly.

Add the wine or lemon juice to the sautéing vegetables and stir 2 minutes longer. Remove from the heat.

Stir in the remaining ingredients, taste, and correct the seasonings.

Cut the squash in half lengthwise. Scoop out the seeds and hollow just enough to accommodate the filling. There are two ways to bake this dish:

1. Fill each half to just level and put them back together holding

(continued on next page)

1 12-inch zucchini, or larger
½ cup uncooked brown rice
¼ pound butter
1 large onion, chopped
½ cup parsley, chopped
¼ pound mushrooms, chopped
2 tablespoons dry sherry, vermouth, white wine, or lemon juice
1 cup tofu, mashed
⅛ teaspoon cinnamon
½ cup raisins
pepper, to taste
paprika, to taste
(salt—optional)

them securely with toothpicks along the edges. Place in a baking dish and cover tightly with a lid or with foil. Pierce the foil.

2. Fill each half with a nice rounded pile of filling. Place the two halves side by side in a baking dish. Dust with paprika. Cover tightly with a lid or with foil. Pierce the foil two or three times to allow steam to escape.

Bake covered for 30 minutes at 350°F. Remove the foil and leave in oven for another 5 minutes.
Yield: 4 to 6 servings

Broiled Tofu Slices

tofu, sliced ¾ inch thick
Okara Fry-and-Bake
   Coating (page 87)
Your choice of topping
- soy sauce
- teriyaki sauce
- mozzarella cheese,
   sliced thin

Broiled tofu takes on an unusual chewy texture. Firm pieces can be skewered for shish kebab.

Slice the tofu ¾ inch thick and dredge in a coating, if you wish, or just brush with any of the sauces mentioned or use both. You might try topping the slices with mozzarella cheese. Arrange on an oiled broiler pan. You can also use a charcoal broiler, a hibachi, or if the tofu is very firm, slide cubes on a skewer. Broil until the slices become brown and crusty. Turn and brown the other side.

You'll find that the slices puff up and the inside texture is rather chewy and unusual. The slices can be eaten as they are or with any kind of sauce.

Deep-Fried Sesame Tofu

A deep-fried delight with Sweet-and-Sour Sauce or the following Pesto Sauce.

Cut the tofu into squares of 1 x ½ x ½ inch. Mix the sesame seeds, cornstarch, and flour. Roll the cubes of tofu in the mixture until they are well coated, and set them on a paper towel until you are ready to cook them.

Heat the oil in a large flat-bottom skillet or use a french fryer if you have one. Fry the tofu cubes until they are well browned. Drain on paper towels and set aside.

1½ cups (1 pound) tofu
½ cup sesame seeds
2 tablespoons cornstarch
3 tablespoons whole wheat flour
¼ to ½ cup oil
(salt—optional)

SWEET-AND-SOUR SAUCE

Mix the cornstarch with the soy sauce and vinegar. When it is smooth, add the tomato sauce and stir well.

Mix pineapple juice (from draining pineapple) with whey or water to total 1½ cups. Stir in the honey and seasonings. Mix these ingredients with those above and heat in a heavy saucepan until thickened. Set aside.

Sauté the green pepper, carrot, and onion in the oil. Add the other ingredients, except for the nuts, and stir well. Add the Sweet-and-Sour Sauce and heat to boiling. Remove from the heat. Top with the warm sesame tofu and sprinkle with the cashews.

Serve with rice and a dry white wine or try sesame tofu with the Pesto Sauce below.

Yield: 5¼ cups

(continued on next page)

¼ cup cornstarch or arrowroot
¼ cup soy sauce
¼ cup vinegar
¼ cup tomato sauce
1½ cups pineapple juice and whey, mixed
½ cup honey
½ teaspoon onion powder
½ teaspoon powdered ginger
1 green pepper
1 carrot, sliced as thin as possible
1 medium onion, in chunks
2 teaspoons oil
½ cup jicama, water chestnut, or winter radish, sliced
½ cup pineapple bits (drain if you are using canned pineapple)
¼ cup toasted cashew nuts

2 cups fresh basil
3 cloves garlic, crushed
(salt—optional)
½ teaspoon pepper
1½ cups olive oil (for the
    best flavor, but other oil
    will do)
grated cheese
¼ cup walnuts, chopped

PESTO SAUCE

Blend basil and seasonings together at high speed, adding the oil gradually. Store in a tightly closed container in the freezer.

Use 1 tablespoon of pesto for each person, with fried tofu and cooked whole wheat spaghetti or other noodles. Sprinkle with ¼ cup of chopped walnuts and serve with a tossed green salad and French bread.

Yield: 2½ cups

1½ pounds fresh spinach
    or 1 package frozen
    spinach
2 tablespoons oil
1 cup rehydrated PSP
    (page 41)
1 clove garlic, minced
(salt—optional)
pepper, to taste
1 to 3 tablespoons parsley,
    chopped
½ cup grated Parmesan
    cheese
1 egg
¼ to ½ cup tofu, mashed
¼ teaspoon crumbled
    oregano leaves

Ravioli

The basic dough for this filling is found on page 91. Fillings can be endless in variety, but the following are our favorites.

Wash, clean, and cook the spinach. Drain and chop fine, or cook frozen spinach according to the directions on the package, drain, and chop.

Heat the oil in a skillet and add the rehydrated PSP and garlic. Stir and sauté over medium heat for 3 or 4 minutes. Stir in the chopped spinach and continue cooking until the mixture is fairly dry. (It is often difficult to get spinach dry enough and this will do it.)

Mix the remaining ingredients with the above mixture, taste, and correct the seasonings. Fill the ravioli pasta, being careful to pinch the edges so they do not leak. Drop into a large pot of boiling water. Cook for about 10 minutes.

Yield: about 60 ravioli

Cheese Rarebit

Combine the cheese, cornstarch, and pepper. Process the beer, tofu, and Worcestershire sauce in a blender.

Heat the beer mixture to a simmer, then add the cheese mixture. Cook and stir until very smooth, and all the cheese is melted. If needed, add more beer or water to thin slightly. Serve on toast with sliced tomatoes.

Yield: 2 to 4 servings

2 cups (½ pound) cheddar
  or Swiss cheese, grated
1 tablespoon cornstarch
pepper, to taste
½ cup beer, soymilk or
  dairy milk, whey, or
  water
½ cup tofu
1 teaspoon Worcestershire
  sauce

Tofu Broccoli Casserole

Preheat the oven to 350°F.

Slice tofu into ½-inch slices and arrange with the broccoli in an oiled 8½ x 11-inch baking pan.

Mix mayonnaise, soup, curry powder, lemon juice, and pepper and salt, blend well, and pour over the tofu and broccoli.

Sprinkle Parmesan cheese over the dish and bake for 30 minutes. You may wish to gratiné under the broiler before serving.

Fine companions for this casserole would be a mixture of brown and wild rice, a tossed salad, and crusty French bread. Try a dry white wine with it.

Yield: 4 to 6 servings

1 pound tofu, sliced into
  ½-inch-thick pieces
2 packages frozen broccoli
  or the fresh equivalent,
  thawed under hot water
  or cooked
1 cup egg mayonnaise
  or Tofu Mayonnaise
  (page 105)
2 cups homemade cream
  of chicken soup
2 teaspoons curry powder
2 teaspoons lemon juice
pepper, to taste
(salt—optional)
½ cup Parmesan cheese

Eggplant Casserole Italienne

1 large eggplant, sliced
    into ½-inch-thick pieces
¼ cup oil
1¼ cups tofu, mashed
1 cup grated Parmesan
    cheese
¼ cup parsley, chopped
⅛ teaspoon garlic powder
(1 egg—optional)
½ cup crumb mixture
    (bread crumbs, dry
    okara, and grated
    Parmesan cheese)
1 large onion, sliced very
    thin
1 small green pepper,
    sliced very thin
chopped fresh mushrooms
sliced Monterey Jack
    cheese
1 to 1½ cups spaghetti
    sauce

Brush both sides of each eggplant slice with oil. Arrange on broiler tray or a cookie sheet and broil under high heat until browned. Turn and brown the other side and set aside. (Eggplant has a phenomenal capacity for absorbing oil when sautéed or fried. Broiling involves little oil, while producing a very satisfactory result.)

Preheat oven to 375°F.

Mix tofu, Parmesan cheese, parsley, garlic powder, and egg. Set aside.

To assemble, first sprinkle the bottom of a rectangular baking dish with half of the crumb mixture. Arrange slices of broiled eggplant around the pan and fill the spaces with the tofu–cheese mixture; cover with slices of onion, green pepper, and mushrooms. Sprinkle with remaining crumb mixture. Spread a layer of sliced cheese. Top with spaghetti sauce.

Bake for 45 to 55 minutes or until browned and well blended. Serve with green salad and warm whole wheat garlic bread.

Yield: 6 to 10 servings

Potato–Tofu–Cabbage Casserole

Preheat oven to 350°F.

Place the first 7 ingredients in the blender and process until very smooth. Stir in the grated cheese—do not blend.

Sauté the onions in the oil and add to the tofu mixture.

Assemble the casserole by arranging half of the potatoes and cabbage on the bottom of the casserole, and topping with the cheese sauce. Repeat this layering again. Top with the bread crumbs, and sprinkle with grated cheese. Bake for 35 to 45 minutes or until the cabbage is done.

Yield: 4 to 6 servings

1½ cups tofu, mashed
½ cup soymilk or dairy milk
(salt—optional)
pepper, to taste
1 teaspoon Worcestershire sauce
½ teaspoon marjoram
¼ teaspoon garlic powder
½ cup cheddar cheese, grated
½ cup onion, chopped
2 tablespoons oil
2 large potatoes, cooked and thinly sliced
2 quarts cabbage, thinly sliced
1 cup whole wheat bread crumbs
grated Parmesan cheese

Tuna Tofu Casserole

Preheat oven to 350°F.

Heat soymilk and butter until the butter melts; set aside. Cube the bread and mix with the tuna and flavorings.

Beat the eggs and add the warm soymilk and butter while beating.

Oil a 1½- to 2-quart casserole. Spread half of the bread–tuna mixture on the bottom. Arrange a layer of tofu slices and sprinkle the olives over the tofu. Then sprinkle the wheat germ over the olives, adding salt and pepper if desired. Spread the remainder of the bread–tuna mixture and pour the egg mixture over the whole casserole. Bake for approximately 1 hour, or until puffed and brown. Serve immediately.

Yield: 4 to 6 servings

1½ cups soymilk or dairy milk
3 tablespoons butter
2 slices dry whole wheat bread
1 small can tuna
1 tablespoon onion, chopped
1 tablespoon parsley, chopped
2 eggs
12 ounces tofu, sliced
1 small can black olives, chopped
¼ cup wheat germ
(salt—optional)
pepper, to taste

Tofu Artichoke Casserole with Chicken or Tuna

1⅔ cups tofu (1 pound), drained and sliced

4 pieces boned chicken, or 1 small can tuna, drained

2 tablespoons butter or oil

2 tablespoons whole wheat flour or cornstarch

¼ cup water

1 cup chicken broth or boullion

2 tablespoons cream, sour cream, or yogurt

1 tablespoon sherry or dry vermouth

pepper, to taste

(salt—optional)

¼ pound fresh mushrooms, sliced

artichoke hearts, as desired

You'll like to serve this with bread to mop up the tasty sauce.
Preheat oven to 375°F.

Drain tofu and slice. Set aside for later use. Brown chicken in hot butter or oil, and set aside.

Mix the flour or cornstarch with the water. Heat the broth and add the thickener. Add the cream and wine and seasoning. Taste and correct seasonings.

Stir the sauce into the pan of mushrooms. Mix well to pick up the flavoring of the browned juices in the pan.

Arrange the tofu slices and chicken or tuna in the greased casserole. Arrange the artichokes with the above. Pour the sauce over the top. Sprinkle with paprika. Bake for about 40 minutes, or until nicely browned.

Yield: 4 servings

Tortilla Casserole

Sauté tofu, onion, and garlic in oil until the onions are clear. Add tomatoes, liquid, and seasonings and simmer for 45 minutes.

Preheat oven to 350°F.

Oil a bean pot or casserole. Spread some sauce over the bottom, and cover with a tortilla or two. Sprinkle with grated cheese, chopped onion, sour cream, and chopped olives. Continue to add layers, including sauce, until all the ingredients are gone, and top with a layer of sauce, dollops of sour cream, olives, and green onions.

Bake until heated throughout (about 20 minutes). Spoon over brown rice or wheat pilaf and serve with a tossed salad.

Yield: 5 or 6 servings

1⅔ cups (1 pound) tofu, mashed
¾ cup onion, chopped
1 or 2 cloves garlic, minced
3 tablespoons oil
2 cups tomatoes, chopped
1 cup whey or water
3 tablespoons chili powder, or to taste
1 teaspoon cumin seed
pepper, to taste
(salt—optional)
10 to 12 tortillas
1 cup any cheese, grated
1 onion, chopped
1 pint sour cream
black olives, chopped
green onions (scallions), sliced

Garbanzo Okara Loaf

Preheat oven to 350°F.

Okara enhances the texture of this meatless loaf. Try it for yourself, and go on to using okara in other loaves and casseroles. As a general rule of thumb, add ⅛ cup (2 tablespoons) of okara for each serving the recipe will yield.

Mash or grind the garbanzos or put them through a food processor. Mix with the okara and spinach.

Sauté the onion, carrot, green pepper, and garlic in the oil.

Beat the eggs lightly, and blend in the flour, pepper, and salt.

Add the grated cheese and all other ingredients and mix well. Pour the mixture into a greased 5 x 9-inch loaf pan and bake until set, about 30 minutes.

Yield: 6 servings

2 cups cooked or canned garbanzos
¾ cup okara
1 package frozen spinach, or 1 cup fresh spinach; cooked, drained, and chopped
1 medium onion, chopped
1 carrot, grated
½ green pepper, chopped
(1 clove garlic, chopped or crushed—optional)
1 tablespoon oil
3 eggs
2 tablespoons whole wheat flour
pepper, to taste
(salt—optional)
½ cup cheddar cheese, grated

1 pound ground beef
1⅔ to 2½ cups (1 to 1½ pounds) tofu
1 medium onion, chopped fine
½ cup celery, chopped
¼ cup parsley, chopped
(salt—optional)
(¼ teaspoon ground cloves—optional)
2 eggs
½ cup wheat germ
¼ cup soymilk, water, or wine
⅓ cup sunflower seeds

2 tablespoons oil or clarified butter
2 eggs
½ cup soymilk or dairy milk
½ cup whole wheat bread crumbs
¼ cup wheat germ
pepper, to taste
(salt—optional)
½ teaspoon powdered oregano
1½ cups carrots, grated
½ cup onions, chopped
1 cup mixed green peppers and mushrooms, chopped
¼ teaspoon garlic powder, or fresh equivalent
6 to 8 slices of tofu, roughly 4 inches square and ½ inch thick
any cheese, grated

Tofu Meat Loaf

Made with 1 pound of meat and a like amount of tofu, this dinner loaf allows you to cut meat consumption in half without sacrificing flavor. Your cholesterol consumption will be halved as well.

Preheat oven to 350°F.

Combine all ingredients except sunflower seeds in a bowl and beat with an electric mixer until smooth.

Spoon the mixture, which will be quite moist, into a loaf pan and top with the sunflower seeds. Bake for 1 to 1½ hours and serve hot with a sauce. Save the leftovers to slice cold for sandwiches.

Yield: 8 to 10 servings

Carrot Tofu Loaf

When served along with a salad, this attractive loaf makes a very satisfying meal.

Preheat oven to 325°F.

Mix together the first 7 ingredients until they are thoroughly combined.

Steam the carrots until just partly cooked. Mix the onions, peppers, mushrooms, and garlic with the carrots and add to the egg and milk mixture.

Pour half of the carrot mixture into a casserole dish, and place the sliced tofu in the center. Pour the rest of the mixture over the tofu, and garnish with grated cheese. Bake for 40 to 50 minutes.

Yield: about 10 servings

Carrots Parmesan with Tofu

Preheat oven to 350°F.

Blend tofu, milk, egg, cheese, and seasonings in the blender. Arrange the carrots and sliced onions in a lightly oiled 1½-quart casserole. Pour the tofu mixture over the carrots. Top with cashews.

Bake for about 45 minutes. This makes a nice main dish for a light meal. Serve with a green vegetable or a green salad and fresh whole wheat rolls.

Yield: 6 servings

1 cup tofu, mashed
¼ cup soymilk or dairy milk
1 egg
¼ cup Parmesan cheese
pepper, to taste
(salt—optional)
dash of nutmeg
5 large carrots, sliced and cooked until tender
1 small onion, sliced very thin
¼ to ½ cup cashew nuts

Meatless Chili

This chili is especially enjoyable with a green salad, French bread, and Chianti. Garnishes might include grated cheese, chopped olives, or sliced green onions. Make up extra chili to freeze for another day.

Cook beans and wheat until tender (usually 3 to 4 hours or about 35 minutes in a pressure cooker).

Sauté the garlic and onions in the oil. Add the tofu and cook lightly. Stir in spices and peppers, then add the sauce and tomatoes. If this is too thick (it should be the consistency of a sauce), thin with more tomato sauce. Simmer for about 20 minutes to allow the tofu to absorb the flavors.

Stir the sauce into the cooked beans, then add whey or water until the proper consistency is reached. Simmer gently an additional hour or so. If possible, improve the flavor by letting the chili stand before serving and then reheating.

Yield: 6 to 8 servings

½ cup soybeans
1 cup pinto beans
½ cup whole wheat berries
1 clove garlic, minced
2 medium onions, chopped
2 tablespoons oil
1 cup tofu, cubed
2 teaspoons chili powder
1 teaspoon cumin seed
dash of cayenne (use in moderation, unless you are an experienced fan)
½ teaspoon powdered oregano
1 bell pepper, chopped
1 hot pepper (such as jalapeño or ancho), or to taste
1¼ cups tomato sauce
3 or 4 tomatoes, chopped
whey (or water)

Hot Tofu Tuna Salad

1¼ cups tofu, cubed
1 small can tuna
¾ cup egg mayonnaise or Tofu Mayonnaise (page 105)
2 tablespoons onion, grated
2 tablespoons lemon juice
½ cup cheddar or Swiss cheese, grated
pepper, to taste
(salt—optional)

Variations
- ½ cup pimento, chopped
- ½ cup black olives, chopped
- ½ cup fresh or frozen peas (uncooked)
- ½ cup almonds, peanuts, or other nuts, chopped

½ cup whole wheat bread crumbs
¼ cup wheat germ
sunflower seeds

This soufflélike main dish is also very good cold and sliced for sandwiches.

Unless the tofu is very solid, drain it for about 30 minutes. Cut into ½-inch cubes.

Preheat oven to 350°F.

Drain the tuna and rinse with hot or boiling water, then flake into a large bowl. Stir mayonnaise, onion, lemon juice, cheese, pepper, and salt into the tuna fish and blend well.

Use one or all of the suggested vegetables or nuts, as desired. Combine with the tuna mixture.

When all ingredients are well blended, carefully fold in the tofu cubes to avoid crushing them. Spoon the mixture into a 2- or 3-quart soufflé dish or a flat baking dish. Sprinkle the top with bread crumbs and wheat germ. Sprinkle on more cheese if you wish and a handful of sunflower seeds. Bake for about 45 minutes or until nicely browned and puffy. Serve at once.

Yield: 4 to 6 servings

Corn and Tofu Soufflé

This eggless soufflé can be a side dish or the main feature of a luncheon or dinner.

Preheat oven to 325°F.

Drain and press the water from a chunk of tofu 2 x 2 x 3 inches and cut into ½-inch cubes.

Drain the corn, and save the liquid as well as the corn. Melt the butter in a saucepan and stir in the flour, stirring together for about a minute. Slowly add the corn liquid, stirring with a wire whip. The sauce should be quite thick before it is removed from the heat.

Stir the corn and mixed vegetables into the sauce. Add pepper and salt. Fold the tofu cubes into the corn mixture very carefully, trying not to crush them. They will work best if they remain in chunks. Spoon the mixture into a lightly oiled soufflé dish that has been sprinkled with wheat germ and Parmesan cheese. Sprinkle the remaining cheese and wheat germ over the top.

Bake for 30 to 45 minutes, being careful not to open the oven during the first 25 minutes.

Serve directly from the oven. It will puff nicely and be a bit more stable than an egg soufflé. Serve with a cream sauce and a green vegetable, or tossed salad and whole wheat bread.

Yield: 6 servings

1 cup tofu, cubed
1 cup corn
2 tablespoons butter or oil
2 tablespoons whole wheat flour
1 cup liquid from corn; or add soymilk, dairy milk, or whey to make 1 cup
1 cup mixture of chopped green peppers, pimento, celery, and onions
pepper, to taste
(salt—optional)
½ cup wheat germ
½ cup grated Parmesan cheese

Spinach Soufflé

1 bunch fresh spinach, or
    1 package frozen spinach
2 eggs, separated
1 cup tofu
½ cup yogurt or sour
    cream
pepper, to taste
(salt—optional)
garlic, to taste
pinch of mace or nutmeg
¼ cup grated Parmesan
    cheese
¼ cup wheat germ

Preheat oven to 450°F.

Cook the spinach by steaming lightly, drain as well as possible, and set aside to cool.

Combine the egg yolks and tofu and beat well. Add the yogurt and seasonings and mix thoroughly.

In a separate bowl, beat the egg whites until they form stiff peaks.

Chop the cooled spinach and blend it with the wheat germ into the egg yolk mixture. Gently fold in the egg whites.

Pour the mixture into a lightly oiled casserole dish, top with grated cheese and wheat germ. Place in the oven, and immediately turn oven down to 350°F. Bake for about an hour or until the eggs are set and the top is browned.

Vegetable Soufflé

1 medium onion, chopped
3 tablespoons oil
½ pound mushrooms,
    sliced
3 tablespoons parsley,
    chopped
1 tablespoon dry sherry
pepper, to taste
(salt—optional)
1 cup tofu, mashed
½ cup wheat germ
2 cups cooked, chopped
    vegetables
2 teaspoons cornstarch
1 cup cold soymilk or dairy
    milk
3 eggs, separated

Preheat oven to 350°F.

Sauté the onion in oil until clear. Add the mushrooms, parsley, sherry, and pepper and salt and stir for about 1 minute. Cover and steam for 1 minute.

Stir the tofu, wheat germ, and vegetables into the above mixture and set aside.

Mix the cornstarch with the cold soymilk. In a saucepan, bring the mixture to a boil. Reduce the heat and beat in the egg yolks, one at a time. Cook a bit longer, but do not boil. Fold the vegetable and milk mixtures together and set aside to cool.

Beat the egg whites until stiff. Fold into the partially cooled vegetable mixture. Spoon into an oiled 2-quart casserole or soufflé dish and bake for 50 to 60 minutes. Serve at once with brown rice or wheat pilaf.

Yield: 6 servings

Okara Zucchini Soufflé

Try this for dinner some hot summer evening.

Grate zucchini coarsely and steam with a small amount of water for 7 to 10 minutes. Set aside to cool.

Sauté onion, green pepper, and celery in oil.

Preheat oven to 325°F.

Separate the eggs and beat the egg whites until stiff. With the same beaters, beat the yolks until light, add the okara, and beat well. Add the cornstarch and seasonings. Stir in the cooled and drained zucchini.

Stir in the sautéed vegetables, then gently fold in the egg whites.

Pour into an oiled soufflé dish and sprinkle the top with cheese and wheat germ. Bake for 30 to 40 minutes.

Although not as light and high as a cheese soufflé, this is a tasty, nutritious, satisfying main dish. Serve it with wheat pilaf or brown rice and a cabbage slaw.

Yield: 6 to 8 servings

8 to 10 small zucchini
  (about 1½ pounds)
½ cup onion, chopped
½ cup green pepper,
  chopped
½ cup celery, chopped
1 tablespoon oil
4 eggs
1 cup okara
1 tablespoon cornstarch,
  potato flour, or rice flour
pepper, to taste
(salt—optional)
¼ teaspoon powdered
  oregano
pinch of nutmeg
½ cup cheddar cheese,
  grated
¼ cup wheat germ

Zucchini Entrée Squares

Fast, easy, and nutritious—as well as a new way to use up some of the zucchini that seem to overtake the garden each summer. Try seasoning this with soy sauce.

Preheat oven to 350°F.

Stir all ingredients together until they are well blended, pour into a lightly oiled 9 x 13-inch pan, and bake for about 1 hour.

Let cool for 15 minutes before serving, then cut into squares. Serve with baked potatoes and a tossed salad.

Yield: 4 to 6 servings

4 or 5 medium zucchini,
  grated
½ cup wheat germ
½ cup okara
1 onion, chopped
1 clove garlic, minced
½ cup fresh parsley,
  chopped
⅓ cup oil
½ cup any cheese, grated
1 teaspoon powdered
  oregano
pepper, to taste
(salt—optional)
4 eggs, beaten until fluffy

Lentil Stew

1 cup lentils
4 cups whey or water
½ teaspoon savory or
    marjoram
2 tablespoons soy sauce
½ cup okara
1 cup uncooked brown rice
1 onion, chopped
2 carrots, chopped
(1 small, diced
    rutabaga—optional)
1 zucchini or yellow
    squash, chopped
1 cup tofu, cubed

If you are able to find small orange lentils, mix them with the more common brownish green ones for visual effect.

Cover the lentils with water and cook until soft (about 1 hour). Drain.

Combine whey or water, savory, soy sauce, okara, rice, and onion in a large pot. Add the lentils, and simmer for 20 to 30 minutes.

Stir in the vegetables (add more whey if the soup is too thick) and tofu; simmer until tender.

Serve in a soup bowl with wheat pilaf or brown rice and Peasant Bread (page 116). Coleslaw also complements the stew.

Yield: 6 to 8 servings

Kima (Indian Curry)

1 large onion, chopped
2 stalks celery, chopped
½ green pepper, chopped
2 tablespoons parsley,
    chopped
1 large potato, chopped
1 clove garlic, minced
¼ pound margarine or
    ½ cup oil
pepper, to taste
(salt—optional)
curry powder, to taste
2 boullion cubes
¼ cup whey or water
1½ cups tofu, cubed or
    mashed
1 large tomato, chopped

This is a free adaptation of a proletarian Indian dish ordinarily made with ground meat. Ours is a curry made without hot pepper to suit American tastes. Add pepper if you wish.

After all vegetables are chopped, heat the margarine or oil in a large, heavy-bottomed pan and sauté the vegetables for 5 to 7 minutes until only partially cooked. (The vegetables should be eaten crisp.)

Add curry (to make your own curry, see page 172) to the sautéing vegetables. Dissolve the boullion cubes in the water or whey and set aside.

Add the tofu to the vegetables, stir it in and cook for about 10 minutes over low heat, stirring frequently. Add the tomato and the boullion and cook slowly for another 10 minutes.

Serve the kima over rice. The vegetables still should be somewhat crisp. If the kima is too watery for your taste, add 1 or 2 teaspoons of cornstarch dissolved in cold water; there should not be very much sauce or juice with this dish, as it is meant to be fairly dry. You might also add chopped olives, chopped walnuts, peanuts, or raisins.

Yield: 4 to 6 servings

Tofu Enchiladas

Chop the vegetables and sauté in the oil until the onions are clear.

Add the tofu, pepper, salt, and chili powder to the sautéed vegetables and continue cooking and stirring until the tofu is fairly dry. Remove from the heat.

Stir in the olives and the wheat germ. Set this mixture aside.

The tortillas may be softened in two ways: either heat in a lightly greased pan just until they are soft and manageable, or steam in a covered pan with the tortillas well elevated above a small amount of water.

Fill softened tortillas with 2 or 3 tablespoons of tofu mixture and roll them up. Arrange them side by side, touching, in a greased 10 x 13-inch baking pan.

Sprinkle the corn over the top of the rolled filled tortillas. Pour the Enchilada Sauce over the top and then sprinkle the cheese. Place in a 350°F oven until it is a golden amalgam of all the ingredients.

Yield: 12 enchiladas

2 large onions, chopped
1 or 2 green peppers, chopped
¼ cup oil
1½ cups tofu, mashed
pepper, to taste
(salt—optional)
1 tablespoon chili powder (or more to taste)
1 can black olives, chopped
(¼ cup wheat germ—optional)
12 tortillas
1½ cups corn
1½ cups Enchilada Sauce
1 cup strong cheese (such as cheddar or Swiss), grated

Enchilada Sauce

QUICK, UNCOOKED SAUCE

Mix all ingredients together well and use as is (or if you wish, heat to boiling and simmer for a few minutes).

Yield: 2 cups

(continued on next page)

2 cups tomato sauce
1 tablespoon vinegar
1 tablespoon chili powder
cayenne pepper, to taste, or a few drops of Tabasco

QUANTITY SAUCE

5 quarts tomatoes, peeled
  and diced
1 cup green pepper,
  chopped
4 onions, finely chopped
2 cups vinegar
⅓ cup honey
(salt—optional)
2 or more small hot
  peppers or
  4 tablespoons
  chili powder
2 teaspoons ground
  allspice
2 teaspoons cinnamon
2 teaspoons cloves
2 teaspoons nutmeg

Spices can be varied to taste. Combine ingredients and heat gradually to boiling. Reduce the heat and simmer for an hour.

While still hot, pack into sterilized canning jars and seal with mason lids. Boil the jars for 10 minutes in a hot water bath, making sure that the water completely covers the tops. Allow to cool, tighten the rings, and store in a cool place.

Yield: 5 pints (1½ to 2 cups needed for Tofu Enchiladas recipe)

Mushrooms à la Crème Tofu

1 pound fresh mushrooms
2 tablespoons butter
2 tablespoons dry sherry
6 English muffins

Sauce
½ cup tofu
½ cup sour cream
½ cup yogurt
1 teaspoon cornstarch
½ cup Parmesan cheese
pepper, to taste
(salt—optional)

This one should become a favorite with mushroom lovers.

Clean, slice, and sauté the mushrooms in the butter for no more than 2 minutes. Add the sherry and cook 1 minute more, stirring constantly.

Process the sauce ingredients in a blender and add to the mushrooms. Cook until thick. Serve on toasted English muffins. The menu for this dinner can be completed by serving a green vegetable and a salad of cucumber slices marinated in yogurt.

The key to this recipe is to work fast. If you have the second group of ingredients ready before you begin to sauté the mushrooms, you can get the whole preparation assembled before the mushrooms start to "bleed." That sounds awful, but you have probably had the disappointing experience of sautéing mushrooms to perfection and setting them aside, only to find that the moisture has seeped out of the mushrooms. To avoid this, prepare this dish at the very last minute and serve it immediately.

Yield: 6 servings

Shrimp and Tofu

Press the tofu on a slanted board and cube (or parboil and dry on a paper towel).

Melt the butter over low heat and add the seasonings. Sauté the tofu cubes for about 10 minutes until slightly brown.

Cut the shrimp into small pieces and add to the tofu. Stir only long enough to heat the shrimp thoroughly.

Cover each slice of bread with slices of cheese. Spoon the tofu and shrimp mixture on top. This makes a perfect dinner served with a vegetable and a tossed salad.

Yield: 4 servings

1¼ cups (12 ounces) tofu, cubed
4 tablespoons butter
¼ teaspoon garlic powder
⅛ teaspoon powdered oregano
pepper, to taste
(salt—optional)
¼ to ½ pound shrimp
4 slices whole wheat toast
sliced cheese (Monterey Jack, Swiss, or cheddar)

Variations
Instead of or in addition to shrimp, add:
- ¼ pound sautéed fresh mushrooms
- chopped or sliced olives
- ¼ cup sunflower seeds, sautéed with tofu

Okara–Mushroom–Shrimp Curry Patties

1 tablespoon onion,
   chopped
1 tablespoon green
   pepper, chopped
5 large mushrooms,
   chopped
1 tablespoon butter
1 tablespoon whole wheat
   flour
2 tablespoons wheat germ
¾ cup okara
1 egg or ¼ cup tofu
½ to 1 teaspoon curry
   powder, or to taste
pepper, to taste
(salt—optional)
10 to 20 small shrimp,
   chopped or mashed
oil, for frying

Sauté the onion, green pepper, and mushrooms in the butter for about 5 minutes.

Mix the flour, wheat germ, okara, and egg or tofu together well, and add the sautéed vegetables.

Mix in the spices and shrimp. Form into patties and refrigerate for a half hour before cooking.

Fry the patties in hot oil until they are brown and crusty. Serve plain or with a cream sauce.

Yield: 4 patties

Tofu à la Newburg

4 tablespoons butter
1 medium onion, chopped
   fine
1 tablespoon green onion
   (scallion) tops, chopped
   fine
1 clove garlic, minced fine
2 tablespoons whole
   wheat flour
1½ cups soymilk or dairy
   milk
1 large green pepper,
   minced
1 teaspoon parsley,
   minced
¼ teaspoon thyme
pinch of cayenne pepper
(salt—optional)
¼ cup dry sherry
1½ cups tofu, cubed
2 slices whole wheat toast

Melt the butter in a saucepan. Add onion and garlic and sauté over medium heat until the onions are clear but not browned. Stir in the flour.

Add the milk and stir until smooth. Add green pepper, parsley, and seasonings and cook for several minutes; the pepper should be quite crisp.

Stir in the sherry, then add the tofu, taking care to fold it in gently so that it does not break up. Heat only until hot and serve immediately.

Serve over pieces of whole wheat toast with tiny green peas and a leafy salad.

Yield: 2 servings

Tofu Noodles Romanov

A creamy, satisfying dinner dish that is easy to prepare.
Preheat oven to 350°F.

Cook the noodles, drain, and blanch with cold water. Parboil the mushrooms by dropping them into boiling, salted water. Allow to return to a boil and cook for 2 minutes. Drain and set aside.

Combine the tofu, sour cream, mayonnaise, grated cheese, onion, salt, garlic powder, and soy sauce and set aside.

Mix the wheat germ and okara and sprinkle them over the bottom of an oiled casserole or flat baking dish.

Spread the cooked noodles evenly in the casserole dish. Arrange the mushrooms and artichokes on top. Cover with the tofu mixture. Sprinkle with grated cheese. Bake for about 40 minutes.

Yield: 6 to 8 servings

1 pound whole wheat noodles
½ pound fresh mushrooms, whole or sliced
1 cup tofu, mashed
1 cup sour cream
½ cup egg mayonnaise or Tofu Mayonnaise (page 105)
1 cup cheese, Swiss or cheddar, grated
3 tablespoons onions, grated
(salt—optional)
¼ teaspoon garlic powder
¼ teaspoon soy sauce
¼ cup wheat germ
¼ cup dried okara
(6 to 8 artichoke hearts—optional)
2 tablespoons grated Parmesan or Romano cheese

Almond–Vegetable–Tofu Sauté

Combine water, cornstarch, soy sauce, chicken stock, and garlic. Set aside.

Stir-fry the carrots and beans in oil over fairly high heat for 2 minutes. Add the cauliflower and onion and stir 1 or 2 minutes longer. Then add the sauce mixture and cook until thickened. The vegetables will be crisp. If you like them softer, cover and cook a bit longer.

Add the tofu and cook just until warmed. Sprinkle almonds over the dish before serving. Serve immediately, with brown rice. For variety, top with roasted cashews or roasted peanuts—this changes the flavor considerably.

Yield: 4 to 6 servings

1 cup water
2 teaspoons cornstarch
2 tablespoons soy sauce
2 teaspoons chicken stock base, or 2 boullion cubes
¼ teaspoon garlic powder, or 1 clove garlic, crushed
1 cup carrots, thinly sliced
1 cup green beans, cut small
2 tablespoons oil
1 cup cauliflower, sliced
1 onion, sliced
1 cup tofu, cubed
½ cup roasted almonds

Dow-Foo Chow Yoke (Stir-Fried Tofu)

⅓ cup tofu, cubed, for
   each serving
1 tablespoon cornstarch
3 tablespoons soy sauce
½ cup cold whey, or water
1 to 2 tablespoons oil
1 clove garlic, mashed or
   pressed
1 cup onions, sliced
½ cup mushrooms, sliced
½ cup soup stock, whey,
   white wine, or any
   mixture of these
½ teaspoon fresh ginger,
   chopped

A good basic recipe to try out in the wok you got for Christmas.

If the tofu is soft, drain it on an inclined surface covered by a clean tea towel or pad of folded paper towels. Press the tofu with a flat weight of some sort (such as a one-pound can over a plate) for 15 minutes or so. Cut the pressed cakes into 1-inch cubes. Mix cornstarch, soy sauce, and liquid together well and set aside.

Heat the oil in a wok, and when the oil is very hot, stir-fry the garlic for about 1 minute. Add the tofu cubes and stir-fry until they are browned.

Add the onions, mushrooms, soup stock, and ginger. Cover and cook for 3 to 5 minutes. Add the cornstarch mixture and stir-fry until the mixture thickens.

Serve with brown rice. Feel free to stir in beef, pork, chicken, or seafood. A number of vegetables make great additions to a stir-fry, including broccoli, cauliflower, tomatoes, thinly sliced squash or zucchini, and cabbage.

Tamale Pie

1 cup cornmeal
1 cup cold water or whey
3 cups boiling water
1 large onion, chopped
1 green pepper, chopped
½ cup celery, chopped
1 large clove garlic,
   pressed or chopped
½ cup parsley, chopped
¼ cup oil

This is a perfect one-dish meal to serve with a green salad and Okara Flatbread (recipe on page 126).

Preheat oven to 350°F.

Combine the cornmeal with the cup of water in a large bowl. Mix well, and then add the boiling water. Cook over boiling water in a double boiler or in a heavy-bottomed saucepan until the cornmeal is well thickened (about 30 minutes). Spread ½ to ⅔ of the cooked meal over the bottom of a deep baking dish that has been greased. Allow it to cool, and set remaining mush aside for later use.

Sauté onion, pepper, celery, garlic, and parsley in the oil until the onions begin to look clear.

(continued)

Add the combination of ground beef (or tofu), okara, and oil to the vegetables and sauté for a few minutes longer.

Add remaining ingredients and simmer for about 10 minutes. Stir occasionally to be sure ingredients are well blended.

Pour all of the above simmered ingredients over the base of cornmeal mush. Cover with the reserved mush. Bake for 45 minutes or until the pie is brown, bubbly, and blended.

Yield: 6 servings

Add to sautéing vegetables one of the following
- ½ pound ground beef, 1 cup okara, and ¼ cup oil

  or
- ¼ pound ground beef, 1¼ cups okara, and ¼ cup oil

  or
- 1 cup mashed tofu and 1 cup okara

2 cups cooked tomatoes
¼ to 1 cup olives, whole or minced
pepper, to taste
(salt—optional)
1 to 3 tablespoons chili powder
1 teaspoon ground coriander

Okara Meat Croquettes

This is a wonderful way to use leftover meat, fowl, or fish when you have just a little and want to feed a whole family.

Sauté onion in oil until clear. Add milk and the meat mixture to the sautéed onion and mix well.

Stir okara, flour, butter, parsley, and seasonings into the above mixture; when it is thoroughly blended and heated, remove from the heat and add the egg, beating it in well. Cook for 1 more minute, stirring constantly.

Remove from the fire and spread on a platter to cool. Cut when cool and firm and shape into 3-inch-long cylinders, into fritters, or into any shape you desire. Roll in crumbs (the mixture will hold together better if it has been refrigerated for an hour) and fry in deep fat or in a frying pan with a generous amount of oil until they are golden brown.

Serve with your favorite sauce.

Yield: 8 to 10 croquettes

½ medium onion, minced
1 tablespoon oil
½ cup soymilk or dairy milk
1 cup of the following, alone or in combination
leftover meat, ham, chicken, turkey, or fish, plus cooked rice, hominy, or mashed potato to total 1 cup
1 cup okara
⅛ to ¼ cup whole wheat flour
2 tablespoons butter or oil
2 tablespoons parsley, chopped
pepper, to taste
(salt—optional)
pinch of nutmeg
1 beaten egg

2 tablespoons cornstarch
½ cup cold soymilk or
    dairy milk
(salt—optional)
1 or 2 eggs
½ cup cottage cheese
½ cup yogurt
1 cup tofu
pepper, to taste
dash of freshly ground
    nutmeg
dash of Worcestershire
    sauce

Your options
- ½ to 1 cup cheddar,
  Swiss, blue, or
  combination of these
  cheeses, grated
- 1 medium onion,
  chopped and sautéed
  in 1 tablespoon oil or
  butter
- ½ pound fresh
  mushrooms, chopped
  or sliced
- 1 cup any cooked
  vegetable, well
  drained
- ½ cup cut-up shrimp
  or any flaked fish,
  with 1 tablespoon dry
  sherry
- herbs, to taste

Tofu Quiche

A quiche can be served as a full dinner accompanied by a salad and stout bread and perhaps preceded by a soup. Our quiche has few eggs and lots of tofu, and the proportions can be varied at will.

Use the quiche pie crust that follows.

Preheat oven to 350°F.

Combine cornstarch, milk, and salt in a blender and process until smooth. Add the remaining ingredients and process until very smooth.

Stir in your choice from the cheese, vegetable, and shrimp options. Pour into the baked quiche shell (recipe follows), and bake for about 35 to 40 minutes, until a knife inserted into the middle comes out clean. If the quiche is not brown, place under the broiler for a few minutes, or until nicely browned. Let stand for about 5 minutes before cutting.

Yield: 6 to 8 servings

Vegetable Quiche

Preheat oven to 325°F.

Okara is at home in vegetable soufflés and in quiches. Add ⅛ cup (2 tablespoons) for each serving the recipe will yield.

Sauté the onion, green pepper, broccoli, and mushrooms in the oil until the onions are clear. Cover and cook for 2 minutes longer. Stir in the corn.

Beat the eggs well, and slowly add the hot milk. Beat in the cornstarch and water mixture. Add the cheese, okara, and flavorings and stir well.

Place the sautéed vegetables in the following crust. Pour the egg mixture over the top, and sprinkle with grated Parmesan cheese. Bake until a knife inserted into the custard comes out clean.

Yield: 6 to 8 servings

1 medium onion, sliced thin
½ green pepper, chopped
1 cup broccoli, chopped
1 cup mushrooms, sliced
1 tablespoon oil
1 cup corn
4 eggs
2 cups scalded soymilk or dairy milk
1 tablespoon cornstarch mixed with 2 tablespoons cold water
1 cup grated cheese (cheddar, Monterey Jack, Swiss, or mixed)
¾ cup okara
(salt—optional)
pinch of nutmeg
pepper, to taste
½ teaspoon Worcestershire sauce
grated Parmesan cheese

Pie Shell for Quiche

Note that this is not a crust for sweet dessert pies. Preheat oven to 325°F.

Mix the dry ingredients well. Blend margarine, butter, or oil into the above mixture.

Pat into a quiche pan or a pie pan. Quiche pans have straight sides so try to press the crumbs up the sides of the pan. (A pie pan does just as well.) Bake for 10 to 20 minutes, or until the crust is just beginning to brown. Fill with quiche mixture, and bake according to recipe specifications.

Yield: 1 crust

1 cup crumbs
½ cup okara
(salt—optional)
¼ cup grated Parmesan or other dry cheese
¼ teaspoon paprika
3 tablespoons melted butter, margarine, or oil

Green Peppers Stuffed with Tofu

4 sweet peppers
1 onion, chopped
1 small stalk celery,
 chopped
1 slice of nitrite-free bacon,
 or 1½ tablespoons oil
1 cup tofu, mashed
¼ cup wheat germ
¼ cup any cheese, grated
½ cup black olives,
 chopped
pepper, to taste
(salt—optional)
½ teaspoon curry powder
½ cup whole wheat bread
 crumbs
¼ cup Parmesan cheese
1 tablespoon oil

Green peppers can be filled with many combinations of tofu and vegetables, grains, meat, or seafood.

Cut off the tops of the peppers, remove the seeds and membranes, and parboil the cleaned peppers for about 10 minutes, until nearly done but still crisp. Chop the pepper tops and set aside.

Sauté the onion, celery, and pepper tops in the oil until tender; if using bacon, fry it until crisp, remove, and sauté vegetables in the fat until tender.

Mix tofu, wheat germ, cheese, olives, and seasonings, and stir in the sautéed vegetables (and the optional bacon slice, crumbled). Fill the peppers and place them in a baking dish.

Preheat oven to 350°F.

Mix the bread crumbs, Parmesan cheese, and oil and sprinkle liberally over the tops of the stuffed peppers.

Bake the peppers for 20 to 30 minutes. They may be served with a sauce of your choosing, perhaps curry, mushroom, or tomato.

The menu for this dinner can be rounded out with brown rice and a tossed salad.

Yield: 4 servings

Using Homemade PSP

PSP can be made in either a wet or a dry form. Try them both, as they have different textures.

WET PSP

Wet PSP is frozen, thawed, drained, and flavored tofu. It must be refrigerated, and will keep for about a week.

This PSP is very low in fat. It can be used without adding oil, which is a boon for dieters, but it tastes and works better if sautéed with oil, stirred constantly over low to medium heat for 3 minutes. Use in any recipe calling for ground meat, either alone or mixed with ground meat.

2 cups wet PSP
¼ to ½ cup oil

DRY PSP—METHOD 1

Drying PSP results in a totally different product, similar to ground meat. This is frozen, thawed, drained, and flavored tofu that has been dried. It can be stored indefinitely and rehydrated as follows.

Soak the PSP in very warm water or whey. Heat the vegetable oil in a skillet and add the soaked PSP (along with any excess water) and stir constantly until all liquid disappears. Adjust the amount of oil as you wish.

1 cup dry PSP
1 cup very warm water or
   whey
¼ to ½ cup oil

DRY PSP—METHOD 2

Mix the PSP with the hot water or whey. Let stand for 15 minutes and then add the oil. This method involves no sautéing.

¼ cup dry PSP
¼ cup hot water or whey
1 tablespoon oil

Dinner Loaf with PSP

1 cup PSP
1 cup very hot water or
    whey
1½ cups cooked brown
    rice
1 teaspoon parsley flakes,
    or 1 tablespoon fresh
    parsley, chopped
1 tablespoon whole wheat
    flour
½ cup olives, chopped
2 eggs
1 small to medium onion,
    chopped
¼ cup oil or butter

Stir the PSP into the water and let it stand for about a ½ hour until the water is completely absorbed. Stir occasionally.

Preheat oven to 350°F.

Combine prepared PSP, cooked rice, parsley, whole wheat flour, and chopped olives in a bowl and mix well.

Beat the eggs and add to the above mixture. Sauté the onion in oil for about 5 minutes over medium heat. Stir into the above mixture and pour into an oiled loaf pan.

Bake for about 45 minutes, or until nicely browned. Serve with a parsley, onion, or tomato sauce.

Yield: 4 to 6 servings

PSP Sloppy Joes

2 cups rehydrated PSP or
    1½ cups tofu, mashed
1 large onion, chopped
1 green pepper, chopped
½ cup celery, chopped
¼ cup oil
½ cup homemade catsup
1 tablespoon prepared
    mustard
¼ cup honey
2 tablespoons vinegar
(salt—optional)
2 tablespoons soy sauce
½ to 1 teaspoon chili
    powder
water or whey, as
    necessary

Sauté the vegetables until clear. Add the PSP or tofu. Stir and continue cooking for about 5 minutes.

Stir in remaining ingredients and cook for another 5 minutes. Taste and correct seasonings. Add only as much water as necessary to get the texture you like.

Serve on toasted open-face whole wheat bread or buns with a tossed green salad.

Yield: 10 servings

Stuffed Cabbage Rolls

You can use PSP or meat in this dish, or varying proportions of both. The preparation is about the same whichever combination you choose.

Mix all ingredients except the cabbage leaves and blend well. Divide into 10 or 12 portions.

Place the filling on a cabbage leaf near the spine end. Roll it loosely, folding the sides over the center. Secure with a toothpick.

In a large Dutch oven, line the bottom with 2 or 3 large cabbage leaves. Arrange the rolls on the leaves and cover with 2 or so leaves.

As in most casserole and one-pot dishes, this one is better on the second day.

2 cups prepared PSP or any mixture of ground meat with PSP to total 2 cups
¼ cup onion, chopped
¼ cup fresh parsley, chopped
¼ teaspoon garlic powder, or fresh equivalent
pepper, to taste
(salt—optional)
¼ teaspoon sage
½ cup uncooked brown rice
2 eggs or 1 cup tofu
10 to 12 softened cabbage leaves (page 81)

COOKING STOCK

Mix cooking stock ingredients and pour over the rolls. Cover and bring to a simmer and cook about 40 to 50 minutes, or until the rice in the rolls is done. You might prefer to uncover the pot and bake the rolls in a preheated 400°F oven for about 10 minutes before serving.
Yield: 10 to 12 rolls

1 cup tomato juice
1 onion, sliced
2 bay leaves
3 or 4 whole allspice berries
1 cup whey
pepper, to taste
(salt—optional)
1 tablespoon paprika
½ lemon, cut into wedges

Tacos

1 cup rehydrated PSP
(salt—optional)
½ medium onion,
   chopped
3 tablespoons oil
1 to 3 tablespoons chili
   powder
taco shells
taco sauce

Filling suggestions
   chopped onions
   olives, sliced or
      chopped
   grated cheese
   hot or green pepper,
      chopped
   minced garlic
   shredded lettuce
   cubed tofu, either
      marinated (page
      135) or not
   sliced radishes
   chopped tomatoes

These tacos are made with PSP. Choose what you like from the list of options, but don't feel limited by it. Try whatever fillings come to mind, traditionally Mexican or not.

Reconstitute the PSP according to the suggestions on page 42. Season with salt, if desired.

Sauté the PSP and onion in oil until the onion is clear. Add the chili powder.

Either buy prepared taco shells or make your own corn tortillas and fry in oil, folded in half, until stiff.

Place the various fillings in separate bowls so that people can construct their own tacos.

Top with Enchilada Sauce (page 63).

Yield: 4 to 6 servings

Carrot Tofu Loaf with PSP

1 cup rehydrated PSP
½ cup cooked brown rice
1 teaspoon dry parsley
   flakes
1 tablespoon whole wheat
   flour
½ cup olives, chopped
2 eggs

The carrot lends a nice, bright color.

Prepare PSP according to instructions on page 41. Combine rice, parsley, flour, olives, eggs, Worcestershire sauce, catsup, and wheat germ with the PSP and mix well.

Preheat oven to 350°F.

Heat the oil in a skillet and sauté onion, carrot, and celery until the onions are clear and fairly soft.

Stir the sautéed vegetables into the PSP mixture. Place into an oiled loaf pan.

(continued)

76

Bake for about 45 minutes or until nicely browned. Serve with a sauce of your choice or just as is for the "meat" course of a complete meal.

Yield: 4 to 6 servings

½ teaspoon
   Worcestershire sauce
1 tablespoon homemade
   catsup
¼ cup wheat germ
2 tablespoons oil
1 small onion, chopped
1 carrot, chopped fine
¼ to ½ cup celery,
   chopped

Chili Con PSP

Prepare PSP according to directions on page 41.

Sauté the onion and garlic in oil in a large skillet until the onion is clear and just beginning to brown. Add the PSP and continue to sauté for several minutes.

Stir in the remaining ingredients and cook over low to medium heat for about an hour.

Serve the chili with dark bread or spoon over brown rice.

Yield: 4 to 6 servings

1 to 2 cups rehydrated PSP
1 large onion, chopped
1 large clove garlic, minced
2 tablespoons oil
1½ cups canned or fresh
   tomatoes
2 tablespoons vinegar
1 teaspoon honey
2 tablespoons chili
   powder, or to taste
pepper, to taste
(salt—optional)
cayenne pepper or
   Tabasco, if desired
3 to 3½ cups (2 cans) chili
   or kidney beans, cooked

Spaghetti Sauce

⅓ cup oil
4 large onions, chopped
2 cloves garlic, mashed or
    chopped fine
1 to 2 cups PSP
3 cups canned or fresh
    chopped tomatoes
3 cups tomato sauce
1½ cups tomato paste
pepper, to taste
(salt—optional)
½ cup parsley, chopped
1 teaspoon oregano
6 whole allspice berries
3 bay leaves
½ cup dry red wine
1 teaspoon honey
2 cups water or whey

Spaghetti sauce tastes even better if served the day after you've made it. Store the sauce by freezing it.

Heat the oil in a large heavy-bottomed pot, such as a Dutch oven. Sauté the onions and garlic, stirring often, for about 10 minutes.

Prepare the PSP according to directions on page 41. Add to the onions and stir for another few minutes.

Add remaining ingredients to the sautéed mixture, stir well, and bring to a boil. Lower the heat and simmer for several hours.
Yield: 12 servings

PSP Stroganoff

½ cup onion, minced
½ cup margarine or oil
1 cup rehydrated PSP,
    soaked in 1 cup whey,
    or 1½ cups wet PSP
2 teaspoons dill seed
1 clove garlic, pressed, or
    ¼ teaspoon garlic
    powder
2 tablespoons whole
    wheat flour
pepper, to taste
(salt—optional)
1 cup sour cream
¼ cup yogurt
1 cup sliced mushrooms
(1 cup chopped black
    olives—optional)

Sauté the onion in the oil until it is clear. Add the PSP and continue cooking for about 5 minutes.

Add the dill seed, garlic, flour, pepper, and salt. Stir well.

Mix together the sour cream and the yogurt and add to the above mixture. Stir well and heat thoroughly, but do not boil.

Add the mushrooms and olives and sauté the mixture only until the mushrooms are just heated. Serve immediately over a bed of brown rice.
Yield: 4 servings

Japanese-Style Meatballs

Use meat, PSP, or any combination of the two you wish.

Beat together the meat and PSP, onion, egg, bread crumbs, pepper, salt, and ginger until they are very smooth. Shape into balls the size of a walnut and fry in oil until browned thoroughly.

Serve on toothpicks with the following sauce for dipping.

2 cups ground meat and
  rehydrated PSP, mixed
¼ cup onion, chopped
  very fine
1 egg, beaten
¼ cup whole wheat bread
  crumbs
pepper, to taste
(salt—optional)
½ teaspoon fresh ginger,
  finely chopped

Sauce
4 teaspoons cornstarch
½ cup cold water or whey
1½ cups broth
1 teaspoon soy sauce
¼ teaspoon garlic powder,
  or fresh equivalent
1 tablespoon honey

Dissolve cornstarch in water. For the broth, use beef broth or boullion cubes dissolved in whey or water. Add broth to the dissolved cornstarch.

Add soy sauce, garlic powder, and honey to the mixture, blend, and heat until thickened. Taste and correct seasonings; it should be fairly sweet.

Serve the meatballs as a main dish with the sauce along with bowls of steamed brown rice and a green vegetable.

Yield: 4 servings

PSP Burgers

Either serve these as hamburgers on buns or as patties with a sauce.

Mix all ingredients together, form into patties, and fry in a skillet in a small amount of oil. Fry slowly until very brown and crisp.

Yield: 4 patties

1 cup rehydrated PSP
  (page 41)
2 tablespoons tofu
2 teaspoons wheat germ
2 tablespoons whole
  wheat flour
(salt—optional)
garlic powder or onion
  powder, to taste

79

Skillet Supper

¼ cup oil
1 large onion, chopped
2 cups prepared
    rehydrated PSP, or any
    mixture of PSP and
    ground meat
½ cup celery, chopped
½ cup olives, chopped
½ cup garbanzo beans,
    cooked
½ cup raisins
2 cups tomato sauce,
    tomato juice, or
    vegetable juice cocktail
pepper, to taste
(salt—optional)
½ teaspoon marjoram
½ teaspoon thyme
½ teaspoon rosemary

Heat the oil and sauté the onion until it is clear. Stir in the PSP and meat and continue cooking and stirring until the meat is browned. If you are using only PSP, cook for only 2 or 3 minutes.

Stir the celery into the above mixture and cook for a minute or two.

Add the remaining ingredients and simmer for about 25 minutes. If the mixture is too dry, add a little whey or water.

Serve with pocket bread or corn tortillas. This dish is also good with brown rice and wheat pilaf.

Yield: 4 to 6 servings

Stuffed Grape Leaves (Dolmadakia)

¼ cup oil
1 cup tofu, mashed
½ pound ground lamb
        or
½ cup rehydrated PSP
    (page 41)
        or
1 cup okara
½ cup brown rice
1 egg
1 large onion, chopped
¼ cup water
pepper, to taste
(salt—optional)
5 large garlic cloves
2 fresh lemons, quartered
3 tablespoons dry mint
    leaves, or ⅓ cup fresh
    mint, chopped
1 8-ounce jar vine leaves,
    or softened fresh leaves

Mix oil, tofu and lamb or PSP or okara, rice, egg, onion, water, and pepper.

Take a large pot and place a china plate faceup on the bottom. (The plate should be close to the size of the bottom of the pot.) Peel the garlic, cut the lemons in quarters, and put in the pot with the mint.

Separate the leaves, wash and drain them, and cut off the stems. Place a large teaspoonful of filling at the wide part of the leaf, and form into a closed packet. Arrange them in the pot as they are rolled.

When all the rolls are formed and arranged in the pot, place another plate on top of them, facedown. This is to keep them from bobbing around when they are cooking. Add enough water or whey to almost cover the rolls and cook slowly for from 1 to 2 hours.

(continued)

PREPARING LEAVES FOR STUFFING

Various leaves can be used for packaging fillings, but they must be softened before use. This is a general way to prepare edible leaves.

Carefully loosen cabbage leaves from the head so as not to break the spine. It helps to cut out the stem with a thin, sharp knife.

Wash leaves carefully and drop into boiling water, cooking only long enough for them to become pliable. Papaya leaves may need parboiling to remove bitterness.

Drain the leaves in a colander or on a rack and trim away tough parts before stuffing. Sometimes the spines of lettuce and cabbage leaves are too stiff to make compact rolls. The stems and beginning spine of grape leaves are also tough and unpleasant to eat.

Use the softened leaves for Stuffed Grape Leaves (page 80) and Stuffed Cabbage Rolls (page 75).

Yield: serves 6 to 8 people

cabbage leaves
grape leaves
papaya leaves
lettuce leaves

Pizza Dough with Okara

½ cup warm water or
   whey
½ teaspoon honey
1 teaspoon dry yeast
(salt—optional)
1 teaspoon oil
1 to 1¼ cups whole wheat
   flour
¼ cup wheat germ
¼ to ½ cup okara

Combine the whey and honey and dissolve the yeast in the mixture. Let this stand for 5 minutes.

Add salt and oil and let stand another 5 minutes.

Stir in the flour, wheat germ, and okara, and mix well. Form the dough into a ball and place in a lightly oiled bowl. Set in a warm place until it has doubled in bulk (45 minutes to an hour). Then knead the dough until smooth. If it sticks all over your hands, add some more flour.

Separate the dough into 10 to 12 sections. Roll or press out each one into an individual round of 5 inches in diameter. Cover with the sauce that follows, and bake for 25 to 35 minutes.

Yield: 10 to 12   5-inch pies

Pizza Sauce

1 cup tofu, 1 cup of PSP, or
   a mixture of the two
2 tablespoons oil
1 onion, finely chopped
1 clove garlic, minced
1 cup tomato sauce
2 or 3 fresh tomatoes (if
   available), sliced
½ sweet pepper (if
   available), diced
½ teaspoon basil
½ teaspoon rosemary
½ teaspoon oregano
(salt—optional)

Sauté tofu and/or PSP in oil with garlic and onions until the onions are clear and well cooked.

Add in the remaining ingredients. If you don't have fresh tomatoes, you might want to add a canned one or two. You might also try experimenting with grated zucchini or other vegetables.

Cover mini-pizzas with the basic sauce, and grate cheese on top (mozzarella is the traditional pizza cheese, along with Parmesan, but there's nothing to say that you can't use cheddar and Monterey Jack). At this point you can customize with olives, extra onions, or whatever. Particularly good is thinly sliced tofu, marinated in a soy-based sauce such as the miso sauce on page 135. That's the nice thing about these individual pizzas—each one can be custom-made.

Bake at 375°F for 25 to 35 minutes.

Yield: serves 10 to 12

Side Dishes and Preparations 9

Here's further evidence of the versatility of tofu and its soy relatives.

Side Dishes and Preparations
Tiropeta (Greek Cheese Pie) 84
Kreplach or Pierogi 84
Okara Turkey Dumplings 85
Chinese Steamed Buns (Pao-Tze) 85
Okara Stuffing for Poultry 86
PSP Snack 86
Batter for Deep Frying 87
Okara Fry-and-Bake Coating 87
Tofu Cheese Ball ...…... 88
Filled Puffs (Brandteigkrapfer mit Salziger Fulle) 88
Rebaked Potatoes with Tofu 89
Spiked Popcorn 90
Egg Roll 90
Wonton or Pot Sticker Dough (Whole Wheat Egg Noodles) 91
Pot Stickers (Kuo Teh) 92
Wonton 93

Tiropeta (Greek Cheese Pie)

6 eggs
¼ pound butter
½ pound feta cheese
½ pound tofu (a bit less
    than a cup)
¼ pound filo (phyllo)
    leaves
¼ pound butter

This dish is usually considered an appetizer, but it makes an admirable main dish.

Preheat oven to 350°F.

Beat eggs until thick. Melt ¼ pound butter and allow it to cool. Mash the cheese and tofu in a separate bowl. Add the cooled melted butter and beat well with a hand or electric beater. Add the eggs gradually and beat until fluffy and light.

Cut the filo leaves to fit a 7 x 11-inch rectangular pan (about 2 inches deep). Butter leaves with the second ¼ pound. Line the bottom of the pan with 8 or 9 leaves. Pour in the egg–cheese mixture and top with 8 or 9 more leaves.

Bake for about 30 minutes or until golden brown. Let the pie stand for about 20 minutes before cutting. Serve warm with a green vegetable and a salad.

Tiropeta can also be made as tiny triangular bite-size pies for appetizers. Cut the filo leaves in long strips, buttering each strip, and rolling or folding over a teaspoon of filling to form a triangle. Bake the pies on a cookie sheet for 10 to 15 minutes, or until golden brown. Serve hot.

Yield: 8 large squares

Kreplach or Pierogi

1 medium onion, chopped
    fine
1 tablespoon oil
1 cup rehydrated PSP
    (page 41)
1 egg
(salt—optional)
30 squares Wonton or
    Potsticker Dough (page
    91)

Sauté the onion in the oil until it is clear. Add the PSP to the onion and sauté for 3 or 4 minutes, stirring constantly. Remove from the heat and cool.

Blend in the slightly beaten egg until the ingredients are thoroughly combined.

Fill the center of a 2-inch square of dough with a teaspoon of filling. Moisten the edge with water and fold it into a triangle, pinching the edges well. Drop into boiling soup or water and cook for 10 to 15 minutes.

Yield: 30 kreplach

Okara Turkey Dumplings

Combine the first 7 ingredients with a fork, mashing the okara and blending well.

Add the eggs and stir until the mixture is thoroughly blended. The batter should be quite moist and thick.

Stir the turkey into the batter. If it seems too thick and will not hold together, add 1 tablespoon of hot soup. Drop the batter by spoonsful into rapidly boiling soup. Cover the pot, reduce the heat so the soup will just simmer, and cook for 10 to 12 minutes. Serve immediately.

Yield: 24 large dumplings

Chinese Steamed Buns (Pao-Tze)

These steamed buns with a tofu filling make a quick, easy, and impressive meal.

Sauté cabbage and onions in oil, and stir in the other ingredients. Filling instructions are the same for both recipes.

Separate the biscuits. Stretch them into a larger circle and place a large teaspoonful of filling in the center. Pull and gather the edges together, pinch the gathered edge, and twist closed.

Line a steamer (or other utensil that can be tightly covered) with several layers of wax paper and place the buns about 1 inch apart on top. Place over boiling water, cover tightly, and steam for 10 minutes. Serve hot as a side dish with Chinese food or as an appetizer. They may be made ahead and reheated in a steamer in the oven.

Yield: approximately 16 buns

1½ cups whole wheat flour
1 cup okara
3 teaspoons baking powder
(salt—optional)
2 tablespoons parsley, chopped
1 teaspoon onion powder
pepper, to taste
2 eggs
1½ cups leftover turkey, chopped
your favorite soup

FILLING 1
½ cup tofu, mashed, or rehydrated PSP
1 cup cabbage, finely chopped
4 tablespoons onion, finely chopped
1 teaspoon soy sauce
2 tablespoons hoisin sauce (Oriental plum sauce)

FILLING 2
1 cup cabbage, finely chopped
4 tablespoons onion, finely chopped
½ cup tofu, mashed
3 teaspoons soy sauce
¼ teaspoon powdered ginger
¼ teaspoon garlic powder
¼ teaspoon curry powder
16 uncooked baking powder biscuits (see Okara Bran Biscuits, page 123)

Okara Stuffing for Poultry

½ cup okara
¼ cup wheat germ
2 tablespoons sunflower
  seeds
1½ cups whole wheat
  bread crumbs
pepper, to taste
(salt—optional)
garlic powder, to taste
2 tablespoons raisins
¼ cup celery, chopped
¼ cup parsley, chopped
½ cup oil, melted butter,
  or margarine
¼ to ¾ cup whey, soup
  stock, or water
(1 egg—optional)

Mix all ingredients together. Add the liquid ¼ cup at a time—it is easy to put it in, but impossible to take it out. The stuffing should be fluffy, not too moist.

The egg will improve the texture and consistency of the stuffing, but is not essential.

Stuff the bird loosely in the neck cavity as well as the body cavity. If you like garlic, rub the inside of the bird with a cut clove before stuffing. Stuffing that does not fit can be piled around the bird; it will pick up flavors and enhance gravy stock.

Yield: will stuff a large chicken, a duck, or a turkey fryer

PSP Snack

4 tablespoons butter
1 teaspoon onion powder
1 teaspoon mixed herbs;
  such as basil tarragon,
  rosemary, and thyme
½ teaspoon paprika
1 tablespoon
  Worcestershire sauce
1 tablespoon soy sauce
1 cup dry rehydrated PSP
½ cup peanuts or other
  nuts
1 cup rolled oats
2 cups granola
(½ cup dry
  vegetables—optional)
1 cup popcorn
1 cup broken crackers

Serve in bowls with cocktails before dinner.

Preheat oven to 350°F.

Melt the butter and stir in the seasonings. Make a mixture of any of the remaining ingredients listed to total 4 cups and mix with the seasoned butter.

Bake for 10 to 15 minutes or until lightly toasted and brown.

Yield: 6 servings

Batter for Deep Frying

Here's a batter that spares you the cholesterol of eggs.

Mix the dry ingredients together well, and blend in the okara with a fork until evenly distributed.

Put the tofu, water, and oil in a blender and process until smooth. Pour into the dry ingredients and beat to make a stiff batter.

This recipe will make enough batter to coat about a pound of cut-up fish, meat, prawns, or pressed and fairly dry tofu.

Use about 1 to 1½ inches of oil in a fryer or broad pan and heat to 385°F or just below smoking. Coat the pieces with the batter and lower them into the hot oil very carefully to prevent spattering. Turn a few times and cook until golden brown. Drain on paper towels or a brown paper bag. Serve as soon after frying as possible.

1 cup whole wheat flour
¾ cup cornstarch
pepper, to taste
½ teaspoon paprika
½ teaspoon dill seed
¼ cup okara or whole
   wheat bread crumbs
¼ cup tofu
1 cup water
2 tablespoons oil

Optional dipping sauces
   drawn butter with lemon
      juice
   Japanese-style
      mustard
   soy sauce mixed with
      ginger, wine, and
      honey

Okara Fry-and-Bake Coating

You can store this shake coating, keeping it on hand for whenever you want to add appeal to tofu slices, fish fillets, or meat cutlets.

Mix the ingredients. The texture should be dry, but it should hold together when pressed, if not, add a few more drops of oil. If too oily, add more dry ingredients. Place however much you need in a plastic bag and shake fish or cutlets to coat. With more delicate tofu slices, it is best to spread the coating on wax paper and press moist slices of tofu into the coating.

Refrigerate what you do not use in an airtight container. Do not save leftover used coating, especially from meats or fish.
Yield: 2¼ cups

¼ cup oil
½ cup dried okara
½ cup bread or cracker
   crumbs
¼ cup cornstarch
¼ cup whole wheat flour
¼ cup wheat germ
¼ cup unprocessed bran
paprika, to taste
pepper, to taste

Add any of these you care to
   ¼ teaspoon onion or
      garlic powder
   ½ teaspoon curry
      powder
   ¼ cup grated
      Parmesan cheese or
      other grated cheese
   ¼ cup sesame seeds

Tofu Cheese Ball

This festive recipe is so good that you may find yourself making it for everyday meals. Try the cheese with the cracker recipes on pages 124–25.

Mix everything together and form into a ball. Chill. Garnish with parsley, and sprinkle with chopped walnuts, if desired.

Yield: 2   4-inch balls

1 cup black olives, chopped
½ pound cream cheese, softened
2 cups tofu, or more to achieve proper consistency
1 tablespoon soy sauce
1 tablespoon dry mustard
2 cups cheddar cheese, grated
1 cup Monterey Jack or Muenster cheese, grated
chopped parsley
1 teaspoon Tabasco sauce
(1 tablespoon Worcestershire sauce—optional)

Filled Puffs
(Brandteigkrapfer mit Salziger Fulle)

These little mouthfuls make a delightful appetizer.

Bring the whey to a boil and add butter. In a bowl, beat the egg and add the tofu. Continue beating until the mixture is smooth.

Add flours to the water–butter mixture and stir to make a thick paste. Remove from the heat, place over a pan of cold water, and continue to stir to make a thick paste. Stir in the egg–tofu mixture. Beat by hand until smooth and elastic.

Let the mixture stand for about an hour. On a lightly oiled baking sheet, drop the mixture by the teaspoonful, about 2 inches apart. It will probably be necessary to either grease the spoons or dip them in cold water between uses. Brush with egg white and sprinkle with caraway seeds, poppy seeds, or paprika.

Bake in a preheated 350°F oven for about 10 minutes, and turn heat off (do not open door). Keep the puffs in the oven until they are cool. Remove them from the oven and fill them through a slit.

Yield: 15 to 30 puffs

1 cup water or whey
⅓ cup butter
1 egg
½ cup tofu, mashed
1 cup whole wheat pastry flour
1 tablespoon gluten flour
egg whites
caraway seeds
poppy seeds
paprika

88

(continued)

For fillings we suggest any tofu dip, Liptauer (recipe on page 137), deviled ham, chopped olives with cream cheese, egg salad, mashed tofu with cheddar cheese and garlic, curried tofu, or Meatless Chili (page 57). This recipe also makes dessert cream puffs.

Rebaked Potatoes with Tofu ✓

Preheat oven to 350°F.

Cut the top quarter off the potatoes. Scoop out the cooked insides from both pieces and put in a large bowl with the remaining ingredients. Whip with an electric mixer until fluffy. If there is not enough moisture, add milk by droplets.

Fill the potato shells with the mixture and place on a baking sheet. Sprinkle with grated Parmesan cheese. Bake until nicely browned and crusty (about 10 to 15 minutes). Save the potato skin tops—they make great sandwiches!

Yield: 4 servings

4 potatoes, baked
1 cup tofu, mashed
½ cup strong cheddar, grated
pepper, to taste
(salt—optional)
¼ cup melted butter, margarine, or oil
½ teaspoon onion powder, or to taste; 1 tablespoon grated onion; or 1 tablespoon dry onion
grated Parmesan cheese

Spiked Popcorn

popcorn
PSP Snack mix

First cook ¼ cup of popcorn in the regular way, adding melted butter and salt, if desired, when finished.

Then stir in 1 cup of PSP Snack (page 86).

Sit back with a good movie on TV and a Soy Shake.

Egg Roll

1 cup rehydrated PSP
2 tablespoons oil
1 tablespoon dry sherry
2 tablespoons soy sauce
pepper, to taste
garlic powder, to taste
1 cup celery, finely
   chopped
½ cup onion, chopped
½ cup mushrooms,
   chopped
½ pound fresh bean
   sprouts (about 2 cups)
1 tablespoon cornstarch
2 or 3 tablespoons water

Prepare the PSP according to the directions on page 41. Stir-fry the PSP in hot oil for about 2 minutes. Blend in the seasonings.

Add the chopped vegetables and bean sprouts and stir-fry for about 2 minutes (no more).

Dissolve the cornstarch in water and add to the above. Cook and stir until the mixture is thick and remove from the heat.

Egg roll wrappers can be from 5 to 7 inches square, depending on the size you want. Fill the squares with 2 to 4 tablespoons filling, placing it diagonally across the wrapper. Roll the dough and fold the corners to make a neat, well-closed roll. Moisten the edges with water to make sure they stay closed.

Fry in oil heated to 375°F for about 3 to 5 minutes until they are golden brown and crisp. Drain on paper and serve as soon as possible, with your choice of sauce (mustard or plum).

Yield: 12 to 15 egg rolls

Wonton or Pot Sticker Dough
(Whole Wheat Egg Noodles)

If you prefer to make your own pot stickers from scratch (see next page), here is a recipe for whole wheat dough.

Sift flours and salt together into a large bowl. In a separate bowl, beat the water and eggs together. Make a well in the center of the flour and pour the water–egg mixture into it.

Mix the dough until it forms a soft ball. Knead on a floured board for 5 to 10 minutes, or until it becomes satiny and smooth.

Divide the dough into 4 or more portions. If you want to use only a small amount at this time, the dough can be wrapped as it is and frozen for later use. You might, however, prefer to roll out all the dough at one time and freeze or refrigerate it for later use.

If you wish to store the cut dough, the cut forms may be stacked if you dust each one with cornstarch to prevent them from sticking together. Wrap tightly to exclude air and freeze or place in the refrigerator. Allow them to return to room temperature before using.

Roll the dough on a floured board or pastry cloth to $1/16$ inch thick—about as thin as possible. Cut the dough with a knife into squares, rectangles, or rounds of whatever size you need. You can even cut the dough into strips and use them for noodles or ravioli, as the dough is the same.

For pot stickers

Cut into circles about 3 inches in diameter.

For egg rolls

Cut dough into 4- or 5-inch squares.

For ravioli

Cut dough into 2 x 4-inch rectangles which are then folded in half.

For kreplach or wonton

Similar to ravioli (only the fillings vary).

For noodles

Cut into strips the width you want and allow them to dry in a warm place.

3½ cups whole wheat
   flour
¼ cup gluten flour
(salt—optional)
1 cup cold water
2 eggs

91

Pot Stickers (Kuo Teh)

36 wonton

Filling
¼ pound ground pork,
lamb, or beef; or ½ cup
tofu, mashed
2 cups tofu, mashed
1 small onion, chopped
fine
1½ to 2 teaspoons
gingerroot, finely
minced; if not available,
1 teaspoon ginger
powder
¼ teaspoon garlic,
pressed, or ⅛ teaspoon
garlic powder
2 tablespoons soy sauce
2½ teaspoons white wine
or dry sherry
1 cup bok choy, chopped,
or a chopped mixture of
cabbage and celery,
including leaves, or any
other crucifer

This is a shortcut method of making a favorite Chinese appetizer. You can make the wrappers, but it's quite a job.

Place the filling ingredients in a large bowl and mix together well.

Place a spoonful of filling in the center of the wrapper and roll or fold into desired shape. Be sure to wet the edges and pinch them together so there will be no leakage of filling.

Bring 1 gallon of water to a boil in a large pot. Drop the dumplings into the water one at a time and allow them to boil until they rise to the top. Then throw in a cup of cold water and bring to a boil again. Remove the dumplings to dry on a tray covered with paper towels.

You may have to go through this operation two or three times if the pot stickers are crowded: dumplings that don't quite fit comfortably in the pot will not cook properly.

After the kuo teh have drained you can set them aside for later frying or serve them just as they are for a side dish. They are very similar to wonton.

Yield: 36 dumplings

Wonton

Prepare PSP according to the recipe on page 41. Sauté it in hot oil for 3 or 4 minutes.

Add the flavorings and cook for a minute or two, stirring constantly. Taste and correct the seasonings.

If you wish, you may add ½ cup of finely chopped shrimp at this point.

Dissolve the cornstarch in the water and add to the above mixture. Stir and continue cooking until the mixture thickens.

Fill wonton wrappers (3 to 3½-inch squares) with about a teaspoon of the filling. Fold them over into a triangle, moisten the edge, and pinch to seal. These may be boiled in soup as in the Kreplach recipe (page 84), or deep fried.

If deep frying, heat the oil to 375°F and fry 8 or 10 wontons at a time for about 2 minutes until they are golden brown. Drain them on paper and keep warm in an oven set at 250°F until serving time. Serve with mustard or plum sauce as a crunchy appetizer.

Yield: 24 to 36 wontons

1 cup rehydrated PSP
2 tablespoons oil
2 tablespoons soy sauce
garlic powder, to taste
1 green onion, chopped,
    or 1 tablespoon onion,
    chopped
6 water chestnuts, peeled
    and chopped, or to taste
1 tablespoon sweet sherry
pepper, to taste
(½ cup shrimp, finely
    chopped—optional)
1 teaspoon cornstarch
¼ cup cold water or whey

Soup, Sandwich, and Salad

10

Whey makes a good soup stock, and can be used in any of your standard recipes. Okara goes into dumplings and noodles. Cut tofu in cubes and add to soups before serving; the texture will be more interesting, and you'll supplement the protein value as well.

In sandwiches, thinly sliced tofu can substitute for cheese, meat, and even mayonnaise, adding lightness, moisture, and improved nutrition.

You'll find our salads and dressings are light and yet substantial enough to be meals in themselves.

Soup, Sandwich, and Salad

Minestrone	96
Basic Cream Soup	97
Ukranian Borscht	97
Chicken Soup or Broth	98
Clam Chowder with PSP	98
Vegetarian Potato Soup	99
Gazpacho	99
Grilled Cheese and Tofu Sandwich	100
Tofu Tuna Salad Sandwich	100
Tofu in Sandwiches	100

Tia's Tofu Sandwich 101
Waldorf Salad 101
Uncle Perk's Potato Salad 102
Sweet and Sour Salad 102
Tofu–Egg Salad 103
Tabouli (Bulgur Salad) 103
Spinach Salad 104
Oriental Salad and Dressing 104
Tofu Mayonnaise 105
Tomato Dressing 106
Tarragon Tofu Dressing 106
Tofu Dressing Extraordinaire 106
Tofu–Blue Cheese Dressing 107
French Dressing 107
Tofu Tahini Salad Dressing 107
Green Goddess Dressing 108
Low-Calorie Thousand Island Dressing 108

SOUP, SANDWICH,
AND SALAD

Minestrone

¼ cup olive oil
2 large onions, chopped
1 cup celery, including
    leaves, chopped
¼ cup fresh parsley,
    chopped
1 carrot, thinly sliced
3 quarts liquid, any
    combination of stock,
    whey, boullion, or water
    from vegetables
1 cup whole tomatoes
pepper, to taste
¼ teaspoon sage
¼ teaspoon rosemary,
    pulverized
pinch of powdered
    oregano
1 cup cabbage, shredded
1 to 1½ cups kidney
    beans, cooked
1 cup whole wheat
    macaroni
1 or 2 zucchini, sliced
1 cup green beans, sliced
tofu cubes
grated Parmesan or
    Romano cheese

This is a thick, hearty soup.

Heat the oil (for authentic Italian flavor, use olive oil) and add the chopped vegetables. Sauté and stir for several minutes. Turn heat to low, cover, and cook for 5 minutes.

Add stock, tomatoes, seasonings, and cabbage to the sautéed vegetables. Simmer covered for about an hour.

Add kidney beans, macaroni, zucchini, and green beans. Cook for about 10 minutes and then taste and correct seasonings. Cook until macaroni is done.

Serve this soup as a meal with whole grain bread, and garnishes of tofu cubes and grated Parmesan or Romano cheese. A light dessert is all you could want after this dinner.

Yield: 5 quarts (10   2-cup servings)

Basic Cream Soup

Add whatever vegetables your garden is producing, or whatever looks freshest at the market.

Melt the butter and add the vegetables. Sauté until clear and cover tightly and cook for 5 minutes over low heat, or until vegetables have reached the desired consistency.

Add the whey and pepper and simmer for 1 minute.

Mix the flour and water and add to the above. Add the soymilk and simmer for about 10 minutes.

If you wish, serve the soup with cubes of tofu and a dollop of sour cream.

Yield: 8 servings

4 tablespoons butter
2 tablespoons onion, minced
2 cups any vegetable
½ cup celery, chopped
1 cup whey or water
pepper, to taste
2 tablespoons whole wheat flour, or more to thicken as desired
½ cup water
2 to 3 cups soymilk

Ukranian Borscht

Simmer the first 9 ingredients together for 1 hour, strain and discard solid matter. Correct seasonings to taste.

Cut the next 5 or any vegetables and lemon (with skin) into large pieces and add them to the stock. Simmer until soft.

Add macaroni, honey, and vinegar. After cooking, correct seasonings. This soup should be slightly sour.

For a really hearty meal, serve this borscht with sour cream.

Use a beef or ham soupbone for the stock, if you wish. You might also want to add cubed tofu (about a ½ pound) to boost the protein content. The whey stock is a rich source of B vitamins that the soybeans lost to the water in the tofu-making process.

Yield: 6 to 8 servings

10 cups whey
2 cloves garlic, chopped
2 bay leaves
6 peppercorns
¼ cup parsley, chopped (include the stems)
1 teaspoon basil
4 carrots, chopped
1 onion, chopped
3 stalks celery, chopped

4 fresh beets with greens
1 cup cabbage
4 potatoes
2 large onions
2 or 3 small tomatoes or 1 small can
½ lemon
½ cup whole wheat elbow macaroni, cooked
1 tablespoon honey
vinegar, to taste

Chicken Soup or Broth

3 to 4 pounds chicken
    parts, chicken feet if you
    have them
whey to cover (3 to 4
    quarts)
2 stalks celery
1 large onion
1 clove garlic
1 carrot
fresh parsley
pepper, to taste

An old laying hen or a so-called stewing chicken is the best for soup. Scald the feet, skin them, and remove the nails. Cut the chicken up.

Cover the chicken with whey in a large soup pot. Bring to a boil and then simmer slowly for 3 or 4 hours. Add the vegetables and seasonings and cook 1 hour longer.

Strain the soup and skim off as much fat as you wish.

Yield: 6 servings

Clam Chowder with PSP

1 cup wet PSP
¼ cup clam juice (fresh
    broth, from a bottle, or
    from a can of minced
    clams)
1 cup onion, chopped
3 cups raw potatoes, diced
¼ cup oil
¼ cup fresh parsley,
    chopped
1½ quarts whey or water
    including any unused
    clam juice
(1 tablespoon cornstarch
    or more if
    desired—optional)
¼ cup cold water
1 cup or more soymilk or
    dairy milk
pepper, to taste
(minced clams—optional)

We call this clam chowder but you may or may not want to use the clam pieces. If you like the flavor of clams but do not care for the very chewy meat, the PSP will do well mixed with clam juice, and that is the way the recipe is given.

Mix the PSP with the clam juice and refrigerate for later use.

Sauté onion and potato in oil; add the parsley and cover. Simmer without added moisture for 5 minutes over a low flame.

Add the whey or water to the above and continue cooking until the potatoes and onions are done. Add the PSP and clam juice.

For a thicker soup, dissolve the cornstarch in the cold water, add the cornstarch and water and soymilk to the soup.

If you are using clams, add just before serving the soup and only warm them as they toughen when overcooked.

Yield: 8 servings

Vegetarian Potato Soup

Combine all ingredients, except butter and flour, in a large pot and simmer until the carrots and potatoes are tender.

Melt the butter in a frying pan and add the flour. Stir constantly until the mixture is brown. Add 1 cup of the hot soup stock and stir furiously. Add one more cup and stir in well so that there will be no lumps. Add this mixture to the soup and stir it in.

Serve the soup with dark bread for a hearty meal.

Yield: 4 quarts

8 large potatoes, peeled and diced
2 large onions, chopped
1 cup celery, chopped
2 carrots, sliced
½ cup tomatoes
¼ cup parsley, chopped, or 2 teaspoons dry parsley
pepper, to taste
whey to cover 2 inches above the vegetables
⅓ cup cooked oatmeal
3 tablespoons butter
3 tablespoons whole wheat flour

Gazpacho

This cold Spanish soup can be thought of as a wet salad. Gazpacho is especially enjoyable when the weather is just too hot for cooking. And hot weather means fresh tomatoes, a necessary ingredient for a first-rate soup. Our version introduces protein in the form of tofu, elevating this "salad" to the status of a real meal.

Process the carrot, celery, garlic, tomato, and parsley in a blender and pour into a bowl.

Blend the lemon juice, salad oil, vinegar, pepper, cumin, Worcestershire sauce, and tomato and add to the first mixture.

For an interesting texture, stir in sliced and cut vegetables according to taste and availability (zucchini, onion, green pepper, jicama, cucumber, and more fresh tomato). Add the tofu cubes, and refrigerate. Serve cold, garnished with sour cream, parsley sprigs, or finely sliced green onions.

Yield: 6 servings

1 carrot
2 stalks celery
2 cloves garlic, minced
1 cup fresh chopped tomato (or homemade tomato juice)
2 sprigs parsley
juice of 2 lemons
½ cup salad oil
2 tablespoons vinegar
pepper, to taste
½ teaspoon whole cumin
1 teaspoon Worcestershire sauce or soy sauce
1 cup fresh chopped tomato
1½ cups tofu, cubed

Grilled Cheese and Tofu Sandwich

1 or 2 slices of whole
    wheat bread
any cheese, sliced
2 thin pieces of tofu
    (marinated in the sauces
    on page 135, if you like)
butter

You can make these either open-face (with no bread on top), or with bread on top and bottom.

Butter both sides of the bread. Add the cheese and the tofu.

Melt some butter in a frying pan and fry the sandwich in it until golden brown.

If you like, add some tomato, sprouts, or other things that sound good to you.

Tofu Tuna Salad Sandwich √

1 can tuna, drained
½ cup tofu, mashed
1 tablespoon lemon juice
½ cup celery, chopped
1 tablespoon onion,
    chopped
2 tablespoons parsley,
    chopped
½ cup Tofu Mayonnaise
    (page 105)
Swiss or cheddar cheese,
    sliced
8 slices whole wheat bread

Rinse the tuna with boiling water, if you wish to remove the oil, and flake.

Mix the tofu and lemon juice with the tuna.

Stir the celery, onion, parsley, and mayonnaise into the tuna–tofu mixture and taste and correct the seasonings.

Melt the cheese on the bread, either in the oven or broiler. Heap on the tuna salad and a lettuce leaf.

These sandwiches can be served either open-face or closed.

Yield: 4 sandwiches

Tofu in Sandwiches

4-ounce cake of tofu

Thinly sliced tofu is a wonderful sandwich fixing. Use it with meat, poultry, or fish, or by itself with garnishes. Tofu and whole grain bread combine to make a complete protein without meat or cheese.

If the tofu is not firm, drain it on paper towels for about 10 minutes, but do not press. Slice about ¼-inch thick and use on whole wheat bread along with your customary sandwich ingredients.

Tia's Tofu Sandwich

Mix mayonnaise and catsup together and use as a spread, or use Low-Calorie Thousand Island Dressing (page 108) if preferred.

Place lettuce on one slice of bread. Place slices of tofu and tomato over the lettuce. Spread with as much dressing as your diet allows.

1 to 3 tablespoons egg
   mayonnaise or Tofu
   Mayonnaise (page 105)
1 to 3 tablespoons
   homemade catsup
lettuce
1 slice whole wheat bread
   (toasted)
4 ounces tofu, sliced
tomato, if desired

Waldorf Salad

Sprinkle the apples with the lemon juice and tofu and toss lightly.

Add the celery, walnuts, sesame seeds, and raisins and toss lightly.

Mix the dressing with the salad until the ingredients are coated. Serve on a lettuce leaf.

Yield: 6 to 8 servings

2 cups apples, cubed
2 teaspoons lemon juice
2 cups tofu, cubed
½ cup celery, very thinly
   sliced
½ cup walnuts, chopped
2 tablespoons toasted
   sesame seeds
¼ cup raisins

DRESSING

Combine all ingredients in the blender and blend until smooth.

1 tablespoon honey
½ cup yogurt
3 tablespoons Tofu
   Mayonnaise (page 105)
pepper, to taste
buttermilk to thin, if
   needed

Uncle Perk's Potato Salad

3 cups cooked potatoes,
   diced
1 cup firm tofu, diced
3 to 4 tablespoons vinegar
¼ to ½ cup onion,
   chopped
pepper, to taste
1 cup chopped celery,
   cucumber, raw zucchini,
   or other vegetable
½ teaspoon celery seed
¼ cup egg mayonnaise or
   Tofu Mayonnaise (page
   105)
1 teaspoon prepared
   mustard
¼ cup tofu
¼ cup yogurt, sour cream,
   or ¼ cup more
   mayonnaise

Put the potatoes and diced tofu in a bowl, pour the vinegar over them to marinate, and set aside.

Meanwhile, mix the vegetables and seasonings with the potatoes.

In a blender, combine the mayonnaise, mustard, tofu, and yogurt and process until smooth.

Mix the onions and the dressing with the potatoes and other vegetables. Refrigerate.

(So that day-old salad will not become too oniony, you can draw off some flavor by letting the chopped onion sit surrounded by salt for 15 minutes or so. Rinse well before incorporating with the recipe.)
Yield: 1 ½ quarts

Sweet and Sour Salad

1 cup honey
½ cup vinegar
½ cup onions, chopped
1 quart sauerkraut, rinsed
   and drained
1 cup celery, thinly sliced
1 green pepper, chopped
¼ cup pimento, chopped
1 cup tofu
1 to 3 teaspoons caraway
   seed

This can be used for slaw or as a garnish for a meat meal. It keeps indefinitely.

Boil the honey and vinegar together and cool.

Prepare the sauerkraut, celery, green pepper, and pimento and set them aside.

Combine the cooled vinegar and honey mixture with the tofu in the blender. Whirl smooth.

Drain and wash the onions thoroughly. Combine all ingredients in a large bowl. Taste and correct seasonings. Refrigerate overnight before serving.
Yield: 1 ½ quarts

Tofu–Egg Salad

Mash the eggs with a fork and stir in the tofu lightly.

Combine the mayonnaise, lemon, and pepper and add to the egg–tofu mixture.

Serve as a salad, or as a sandwich spread with sprouts or lettuce.
Yield: 2 servings

2 hard-boiled eggs
½ cup tofu, cut in ¼-inch cubes
½ cup egg mayonnaise or Tofu Mayonnaise (page 105)
1 teaspoon lemon juice
pepper, to taste

Tabouli (Bulgur Salad)

Bulgur should be slightly undercooked so that the grains are separate and not mushy.

Chop the celery, green pepper, onion, and olives very fine for consistency with the small grains, then combine with the bulgur.

(To prevent the onion from drowning out other flavors in the salad, you can leach out flavorful oils by placing chopped onion in salt for 15 minutes or so. Rinse well.)

Thoroughly mix the PSP or okara into the grain mixture.

Combine the oil, tofu, vinegar, paprika, and pepper in a blender and process well. Stir the dressing into the grain mixture. Refrigerate for several hours and serve.
Yield: 6 to 8 servings

3 cups cooked bulgur
½ cup celery, chopped
½ cup green pepper, chopped
1 medium onion, chopped fine
½ cup black olives, chopped
½ to 1 cup rehydrated PSP (page 41) or okara
¾ cup oil
½ cup tofu
¼ cup vinegar or lemon juice
½ teaspoon paprika
pepper, to taste

Spinach Salad

1 bunch spinach
½ cup tofu, or more to suit
1 tablespoon lemon juice
pepper, to taste
½ teaspoon paprika
½ teaspoon French
   Dijon-type mustard
2 tablespoons lemon juice
1 clove garlic
¼ cup oil
1 tablespoon water or wine

Optional additions
   finely minced green
      onions
   chopped fresh
      mushrooms
   lettuce as desired
   chopped jicama,
      water chestnuts, or
      winter radishes
   chopped radishes

Wash the spinach, remove stems, and tear leaves into bite-size pieces.

Mash together the tofu and lemon juice, adding freshly ground pepper to taste. Toss with spinach.

Combine the paprika, mustard, lemon, garlic, oil, and water in a blender and process until the garlic is liquified. Toss with the spinach salad and add any of the options listed.
Yield: 6 servings

Oriental Salad and Dressing

salad greens
mung bean sprouts
slivered, peeled water
   chestnuts
toasted blanched almonds
jicama or winter radishes,
   sliced

Make sure you have enough of each ingredient to suit those you'll be feeding. Toss lightly in a large salad bowl or arrange in separate piles on a large platter for dipping.

(continued)

DRESSING

Combine tofu, mayonnaise, yogurt, ginger, and soy sauce in a blender and blend smooth. Add drops of buttermilk if necessary to thin.

Stir parsley, coriander, and onions into the tofu mixture. Do not use a blender, as these ingredients should be in pieces. Serve either as a dip for the vegetables mentioned above, or as a dressing for the salad.

Yield: 1½ cups

½ cup tofu
½ cup egg mayonnaise or Tofu Mayonnaise (page 105)
¼ cup yogurt
small piece fresh ginger
1 tablespoon soy sauce
chopped fresh parsley
chopped fresh coriander (if available) or ¼ teaspoon coriander powder
¼ cup onions, finely chopped

Tofu Mayonnaise

This mayonnaise uses no egg. Pick an oil with a flavor that pleases you. Note that adding the lemon in stages and the oil as slowly as your patience will allow will make a thicker mayonnaise. Store the dressing in the refrigerator where it will keep for several weeks.

Place the tofu and seasonings in the blender and add 1 tablespoon of the lemon juice. Blend at high speed, stopping frequently to scrape down the sides of the jar.

Add the oil a few drops at a time, increasing to a steady stream. When about one-third of the oil is added, add another tablespoon of lemon juice, slowly, while blending. Dribble in another one-third of the oil and then add another tablespoon of lemon. Taste now, adding a bit of pepper if you wish. Continue adding the oil until it is gone.

Yield: 1½ cups

1 cup tofu
1 to 2 teaspoons French Dijon-type mustard, or your favorite
3 tablespoons lemon juice
½ cup oil

1 small clove garlic
¼ cup salad oil
2 tablespoons wine
    vinegar
¼ cup whey or water
½ teaspoon dry basil or
    powdered oregano
¼ cup tofu, mashed
pepper, to taste
1 cup fresh tomatoes,
    chopped or cooked
(salt—optional)

Tomato Dressing

Combine all ingredients except the tomatoes in the blender and blend until smooth.

Press as much juice as possible out of the tomatoes and add the juice to the blender mixture. Blend until smooth. Correct seasonings. Pour into a jar and add the chopped tomato pieces. Shake well and let stand for several hours before using.
Yield: 2¼ cups

½ cup salad oil
3 tablespoons French
    Dijon-type mustard
½ teaspoon tarragon
pepper, to taste
1 tablespoon lemon juice
¼ cup water
¼ to ½ cup tofu, to suit

Tarragon Tofu Dressing

This dressing improves in flavor if left in the refrigerator overnight.

Mix all ingredients in a blender for 1 minute.
Yield: 1½ cups

½ cup tofu
½ cup salad oil
¼ cup French Dijon-type
    mustard
½ teaspoon tarragon
pepper, to taste

Tofu Dressing Extraordinaire

Serve on a tossed green salad or on avocado halves.

Put all the ingredients in a blender and process until smooth. If you like a thinner dressing, add water. Keep refrigerated.
Yield: 1¼ cups

Tofu–Blue Cheese Dressing

By using tofu, you can make an inexpensive blue cheese dressing.

Process the tofu, vinegar, and soymilk in a blender, adding the oil 1 tablespoon at a time. Then blend in the blue cheese and pepper, to taste. Remember, you needn't add much cheese, since tofu provides most of the dressing's bulk.

Yield: 1 cup

½ cup tofu
2 tablespoons vinegar
¼ cup soymilk or dairy
   milk
2 tablespoons salad oil
blue cheese, to taste
pepper, to taste
(salt—optional)

French Dressing

The tofu in this dressing keeps the oil in suspension and cuts the sharp taste of the ingredients.

Process all ingredients in a blender until completely smooth. Store in the refrigerator and shake before each use.

Yield: 3 cups

1½ cups salad oil
½ cup vinegar, preferably
   wine
2 tablespoons water
3 tablespoons lemon juice
1 tablespoon honey
1 teaspoon paprika
pepper, to taste
3 tablespoons tofu
½ to 1 large clove garlic, or
   to taste
(salt—optional)

Tofu Tahini Salad Dressing

Process all ingredients in a blender until very smooth, adding water or whey if necessary.

Yield: 1 cup

4 tablespoons tahini
4 tablespoons tofu
2 tablespoons salad oil
juice of ½ lemon
½ clove garlic
pepper, to taste
water or whey, as
   necessary
(salt—optional)

Green Goddess Dressing

1 cup tofu
½ cup egg mayonnaise or
  Tofu Mayonnaise (page
  105)
1 teaspoon onion powder
2 tablespoons lemon juice
1 2-ounce can anchovies,
  drained
1 tablespoon wine vinegar
1 clove garlic
¼ to ⅓ cup parsley,
  minced
pepper, to taste
½ cup sour cream or
  yogurt

In a blender, blend all ingredients except the sour cream or yogurt until smooth, adding drops of buttermilk, soymilk, or water if it is too thick. Taste and correct seasonings. The green comes from the parsley, so blend it until the parsley contributes its color throughout.

Stir in the sour cream and mix thoroughly. Serve on tossed salad with croutons.

This dressing can be stored in the refrigerator for a week or two, but be aware that the anchovies will get stronger in flavor with time.
Yield: 2 cups

Low-Calorie Thousand Island Dressing

½ cup tofu, mashed
½ cup yogurt
pepper, to taste
¼ cup salad oil, or less
½ to 1 teaspoon prepared
  mustard
3 tablespoons homemade
  catsup or chili sauce
3 teaspoons chopped
  pickles or piccalilli

Blend first 5 ingredients, adding buttermilk to thin if necessary.

Stir catsup and pickles into above mixture. Store dressing in the refrigerator.

If this is too thick, thin with water or soymilk.
Yield: 2 cups

Baking with Okara:
Bread, Crackers,
and Pastries   *11*

Okara stars in most of the recipes, adding moisture, texture, fiber, and protein. These qualities are especially important if you would rather cook without eggs.

Soymilk can be used wherever dairy milk is called for. For higher, lighter bread, add gluten flour at a rate of 1 tablespoon to each cup of whole wheat flour.

Baking with Okara: Bread, Crackers, and Pastries
Rye Bread Sticks 111
English Muffins 111
Mugs' and Kate's Pincushion Rolls 112
Okara Danish Yeast Dough 112
Buttermilk Kuchen 113
Whole Wheat Sesame Buns and Bread 114
Orange Nut Bread 115
Sourdough Health Bread 115
Sourdough Starter 116
Peasant Bread 116
Anadama Bread 117
Irish Soda Bread 117
Nellie Twomey's Soda Bread 118

Wheatless, Eggless, Milkless Fruit Bread 119

Pumpkin Spice Bread 119

Banana–Coconut–Tofu Bread (Eggless) 120

Banana Okara Bread 120

Casserole Dill Bread 121

Quick Coffee Cake 121

Scones with Okara 122

Okara Cornsticks 123

Okara Bran Biscuits 123

Buttermilk Doughnuts 124

Oatmeal Crackers with Tofu 124

Tofu Okara Crackers 125

Okara Flatbread 126

Rye Bread Sticks

These are easy to make. They taste their best right out of the oven.

Dissolve the yeast in the warm water. Mix the soymilk, molasses, salt, and okara together in a large bowl. Add the dissolved yeast.

Add the potato flour or mashed potatoes and beat well. Add enough rye flour to make a stiff dough. If seeds are desired, they should be added at this time also.

Knead on a rye-floured board until smooth (about 5 to 7 minutes). Allow to rise in an oiled bowl for about an hour. Preheat oven to 350°F. Place on the floured board again, and roll into a round, ½ inch thick. Cut into strips ½ inch wide and roll each strip until it's 6 inches long. Arrange on an oiled baking sheet. Without a second rising, bake at 350°F. for about 20 minutes until lightly browned. Cool on a wire rack.

Yield: 2½ to 3 pounds

1 tablespoon dry yeast
½ cup warm water
1 cup soymilk
1 tablespoon molasses
(1 teaspoon salt—optional)
1 cup okara
1 cup potato flour or
    mashed potatoes
3 to 4 cups rye flour
(1 teaspoon caraway seed
    or dill seed—optional)

English Muffins

Dissolve the yeast in the whey. Mix the flour and the salt together and set aside.

Stir together the soymilk, honey, butter, and okara, then add the dissolved yeast. Add the flour gradually, beating well after each addition.

When it becomes too stiff to beat, turn the dough onto a floured board and knead until it is smooth and elastic. Place in a greased bowl and cover. Keep in a warm place until doubled in bulk.

Sprinkle the board with cornmeal and turn out the dough onto it. Roll out to about ¾ inch in thickness and cut either into rounds, which are traditional, or squares, which are easier. Cover the cut muffins on the board and let them rise again for a half hour. Bake on a moderately hot griddle, cornmeal side down, for about 7 or 8 minutes or until brown. Turn and bake another 8 minutes or so.

These may be frozen either unbaked, before the second rising, or after baking.

Yield: 12   3-inch muffins

1 tablespoon dry yeast
½ cup warm whey
3½ cups whole wheat
    flour
(salt—optional)
1 cup warm soymilk or
    dairy milk
2 tablespoons honey
3 tablespoons butter or oil
½ cup okara
cornmeal

Mugs' and Kate's Pincushion Rolls

1 tablespoon dry yeast
½ cup lukewarm water
3 tablespoons honey
⅔ cup melted butter
   (cooled)
(salt—optional)
1 cup okara
1 cup mashed potatoes
1 cup scalded milk
2 eggs, beaten
6½ cups whole wheat
   flour

Dissolve the yeast in the water and honey and let stand for 10 minutes.

Add the butter, salt, okara, and potatoes to the milk, and when cool, add the yeast mixture and eggs.

Stir in the flour, 2 cups at a time, mixing well after each addition. Form the dough into rolls and place on a greased pan. Allow the rolls to rise until they have doubled, then bake at 375°F for 25 to 35 minutes.

Yield: 2 to 3 dozen rolls

Okara Danish Yeast Dough

1 tablespoon dry yeast
1½ cups warm soymilk or
   dairy milk
1 cup okara
1 cup whole wheat flour
2 tablespoons honey
1 cup softened butter
¼ cup honey
(salt—optional)
(1 teaspoon grated lemon
   rind—optional)
3½ to 4½ cups whole
   wheat flour

This is by far the best yeast dough for coffee cakes we've found. The okara keeps it moist and the butter makes it rich. The butter is probably the secret of its success, but it can be made with other shortenings as well, with varying results.

Mix the yeast with the milk and add the okara, flour, and honey. Let the mixture stand at room temperature for about a half hour. It should become foamy from the yeast's activity.

Beat the butter until it is soft and light. Add the honey, salt, and lemon rind, and mix thoroughly. Then add the yeast mixture and beat well.

Add flour a little at a time and beat well after each addition. Beat in as much as your mixer can handle, then stir in the rest.

Add the remaining flour by kneading it on a floured pastry board. Knead for a short time only, until the dough is smooth and shiny.

Place the dough in an oiled bowl and let it rise in a warm place until it is doubled in bulk (1 to 2 hours).

Divide the dough into 2 parts and make filled coffee cakes, caramel buns, or any of your favorite yeast dough pastries using traditional or inspired fillings. The following is a good one to try.

(continued)

COFFEE CAKE

Roll out half of the dough until it is ¼ inch thick. Brush the surface with melted butter. Sprinkle with cinnamon and spread with jam or preserves. Roll the dough into a long form. If you have been using a pastry cloth, it is very easy to lift the edge and let the dough roll itself. If you are using a board, lift the edge of the dough and fold it over for the first turn and then roll it carefully, one turn at a time. Lift the roll onto a cookie sheet and shape as you wish, into a circle or oval—or just leave it long. Slit the top with a sharp knife.

After forming your coffee cakes or what have you, cover the trays and move them in a place free from drafts to rise again. When about doubled, bake in a 325°F oven for 30 minutes or until springy and an even light brown. Cool before cutting.

Yield: 2 large cakes

melted butter, to cover
  dough
cinnamon, to taste
jam or preserves

Buttermilk Kuchen

This recipe further demonstrates the advantages of using okara in yeast doughs. These coffee cakes are rich, moist, and light—and have the added protein and fiber that okara contributes.

Sprinkle the yeast on the surface of the warm soymilk, and then stir it in. Add the honey and set the mixture aside. When foamy, add it to the okara, buttermilk, flour, and honey, and beat well. Set aside to rise for 30 minutes to an hour.

In a large bowl, cream the butter until it is light, then add in the yeast mixture. Add eggs and beat well.

Beat in the salt, baking soda, and 2 cups of flour, blending thoroughly. Gradually add the remaining flour; when you can no longer mix, blend using your hands.

After the dough is thoroughly blended, knead it on a floured board until light, spongy, and rather shiny. It should not be as stiff or heavy as bread dough. Place in a large oiled bowl and allow to rise in a warm, draft-free place until doubled in bulk.

The dough is now ready to be formed into coffee cakes to suit your tastes. The following almond filling is a possibility.

Yield: 3 pastries

1 tablespoon dry yeast (or
  1 package or cake)
1 cup warm soymilk
1 tablespoon honey
1 cup okara
1 cup warm buttermilk
1 cup whole wheat pastry
  flour
¼ cup honey
½ pound butter
2 eggs
(salt—optional)
½ teaspoon baking soda
5 to 6½ cups whole wheat
  pastry flour

(continued on next page)

113

ALMOND FILLING FOR KUCHEN

1 cup ground almonds—
   do not blanch
   (this can be done
   in a blender)
½ cup wet okara
½ cup whole wheat bread
   crumbs (very fine)
½ teaspoon cinnamon
(salt—optional)
¼ cup honey
¼ cup melted butter

Mix all ingredients together with a pastry blender or a fork until they form a paste.

Other good fillings are prune butter (lekvar), and honey, raisins, and chopped nuts. Jelly will not work well.

The procedure for filling is about the same no matter what filling you use. First, divide the dough into 3 (or more) parts. Roll a part out on a well-floured pastry cloth to a ½-inch thickness. Coat the sheet of pastry with melted butter. Spread the filling (or a favorite preserve) over the pastry. Sprinkle in some raisins if you wish, and any spices you desire. Grasp the pastry cloth with both hands and gently roll the dough over and over, forming a long snake. Shape the dough into a pretzel or a circle or loaf, and move to a warm place; cover with a tea towel. Allow to rise until about doubled. Then place on the middle rack in a cold oven. Turn the heat on and bake at 350°F for about 30 to 35 minutes, or until nicely browned.

Whole Wheat Sesame Buns and Bread

½ cup okara
1 cup boiling whey or
   water
2 tablespoons oil or butter
(2 teaspoons salt—optional)
1 tablespoon honey
1 cup soymilk or dairy
   milk
1 tablespoon dry yeast
5 to 6 cups whole wheat
   flour
sesame seeds

Combine the first 5 ingredients in a large bowl, and add the soymilk. After the mixture has cooled, add the yeast and let stand for 5 minutes, or until it has thoroughly dispersed.

Stir in flour and beat the mixture well, until stiff.

Knead the dough on a well-floured board until smooth, adding more flour if necessary. Place it in a greased bowl and let it rise in a warm place until doubled in bulk.

When the dough has doubled, punch it down and knead again for a minute or two. The recipe will make two 5 x 9-inch loaves or about a dozen hamburger-size rolls. For loaves, divide the dough into 2 equal parts and place in greased pans.

For rolls, pat the dough or roll with a rolling pin until it is ½ inch thick. Sprinkle a generous amount of sesame seeds on a baking sheet and carefully place the dough on top. Cut into desired shapes, brush the tops with beaten egg white or water, and sprinkle on sesame seeds. Let rise again until double in bulk.

Bake in a 350°F oven until nicely browned (about 20 to 25 minutes for rolls and 45 minutes for bread).
Yield: 2 loaves or 12 rolls

Orange Nut Bread

This is an egg-free yeast batter bread that is particularly good for people on low-sodium diets as well. Serve as a dessert bread with butter, cream cheese, or preserves.

Cook the orange rind, juice, and honey over low heat until somewhat thickened. Remove from the heat and stir in the okara.

Dissolve the yeast in the warm water and set aside.

In a large bowl, mix the tofu with the honey until well blended. Add the other ingredients (except the flour and nuts), the okara and orange mixture, and the yeast. Beat until thoroughly mixed.

Stir in the flour until just blended. Be careful not to overmix. Add the chopped nuts.

Pour the dough into an oiled 5 x 9-inch bread pan or a round, ovenproof bowl. Let it rise for about an hour or until it is about double in bulk. Bake at 350°F for 45 minutes to 1 hour.

Yield: 1 loaf

grated rind of 1 large
  orange
½ cup orange juice
1 tablespoon honey
½ cup okara
2 teaspoons dry yeast
¼ cup warm water
¼ cup tofu
¼ cup honey
(½ teaspoon salt—optional)
⅓ cup buttermilk
2 tablespoons melted
  butter or oil
2 cups whole wheat flour
1 cup any chopped nuts

Sourdough Health Bread

The baking time of 2½ hours is a bit out of the ordinary; try this bread when using the oven for other things, such as cooking a roast or fowl.

Mix the sourdough starter, 3 cups whole wheat flour, and warm water until thoroughly blended. Let this mixture stand overnight. The next morning, remove 1½ cups of this dough and add it to a sourdough starter jar in the refrigerator.

Add oil, honey, okara, salt, whey, anise seed, and caraway seed to the remaining sourdough and mix well. Begin to add 5 cups flour, about a cup at a time, beating well after each addition. When the dough becomes too stiff to beat, place on a floured board, add the rest of the flour, and knead well. Knead until you are weak, rest, and then knead another few minutes.

Divide the dough into two parts. Shape into loaves and place in oiled 5 x 9-inch or 4 x 8-inch pans. Cover and set in a warm place until almost doubled in bulk. Place in a preheated 450°F oven and bake 15 minutes. Lower the heat to 350°F and bake 1 hour. Lower the temperature again to 250°F and bake another hour. Allow the bread to cool before removing it from the pans.

Yield: 2 loaves

1½ cups sourdough
  starter (see following
  recipe)
8 cups whole wheat flour
1½ cups warm water
½ cup oil
½ cup honey
1 cup okara
(1 teaspoon salt—optional)
2 cups warm whey or
  water
1 teaspoon anise seeds,
  ground
1 teaspoon caraway seeds,
  ground

Sourdough Starter

2 cups whole wheat flour
1½ cups warm water or
   whey
(salt—optional)
2 teaspoons dry yeast
1 teaspoon honey

A batch of starter can last almost indefinitely if it is replenished regularly and kept refrigerated. Each time you bake, the entire batch of starter is used; after the dough has been mixed, you then take out a cup or so for the refrigerated batch.

Mix all ingredients and pour into a 2-quart container. Cover loosely with plastic wrap or wax paper and let stand for about 3 days. It should swell and bubble, then fall back and begin to ferment. By the third day, if all is going well, the starter should be thinner and will smell slightly alcoholic. Place the starter in a closely topped container (not of glass), and store in the refrigerator. It will be ready to use in a day. The longer the starter stands, the more sour it will be.

Peasant Bread

3 medium potatoes
1 tablespoon dry yeast
2 cups warm potato liquid
(salt—optional)
2 tablespoons butter
2 tablespoons dark
   molasses
2 tablespoons anise,
   fennel, dill, or caraway
   seeds, in any
   combination
2 cups rye flour
4 cups whole wheat flour
½ cup okara

Peel and dice potatoes, cover with water or whey, cook until soft, mash, and set aside. Be sure to save the liquid the potatoes were cooked in.

Dissolve the yeast in ½ cup of the warm potato liquid (not too hot, or it will kill the yeast). Add the mashed potatoes and mix well.

Beat in the remaining ingredients and knead on a floured board until smooth (about 15 minutes). Let the dough rise, punch it down, and knead again.

Form the dough into 2 loaves. Bake them on an oiled cookie sheet for round loaves, or place in 2 oiled loaf pans for conventional loaves.

Let the loaves rise until they have doubled in bulk, and bake at 350°F for 40 to 60 minutes, or until done.

This hearty bread goes well with soup (try the Minestrone on page 96 or the Ukranian Borscht on page 97). You might care to add a salad to round out the meal.
Yield: 2 loaves

Anadama Bread

Bring the whey or water to a boil in a saucepan. Gradually add cornmeal, stirring constantly. Add salt and okara and mix in well. Pour into a large mixing bowl.

Stir molasses and butter into the above mixture while it is still hot. Cool to lukewarm. Disperse the yeast in the warm water and add it to the lukewarm mixture.

Mix in about 2 cups of the flour and the wheat germ. Beat very well, until the dough begins to creep up the beaters. Stir and mix in the remainder of the flour until the dough is smooth and elastic; this will take 5 to 20 minutes, depending on your strength.

Let the dough rise in a warm, draft-free place until doubled in bulk. Punch it down and return it to the floured board. Form into a loaf and place in a 5 x 9-inch loaf pan. Let rise again until doubled. Brush the top with melted butter, sprinkle with cornmeal, and place in a 350° to 375°F oven for 30 to 40 minutes, or until nicely browned.
Yield: 1 loaf

1½ cups whey or water
¼ cup yellow cornmeal
(1 teaspoon salt—optional)
⅜ cup okara
¼ cup molasses
1 tablespoon butter
1 tablespoon dry yeast or
    1 cake yeast
3 tablespoons warm water
3½ cups whole wheat
    flour
3 tablespoons wheat germ

Irish Soda Bread

Mix the flour, baking soda, and salt. Cut in the butter or mix in the oil until the ingredients resemble a coarse meal.

Then mix in the raisins and the caraway seeds.

Combine the honey, buttermilk, and okara, and gradually add them to make dough—this recipe should make a rather soft dough. Form into 2 slightly flattened round loaves. Brush the tops with melted butter or egg white or yolk. Cut a cross in the tops of the loaves.

Bake immediately on an oiled cookie sheet for about 1 hour or until the bread is nicely browned. Serve warm with butter and preserves for a snack, for afternoon tea, or with a light lunch or supper.
Yield: 2   6-inch round loaves

4 cups whole wheat flour
1 teaspoon baking soda
(1 teaspoon salt—optional)
¾ cup butter or ⅔ cup oil
1 cup raisins or currants
1 tablespoon caraway
    seeds
⅔ cup honey
1⅓ cups buttermilk or
    soured soymilk
½ cup okara

2 eggs
1½ cups buttermilk or
   soured soymilk
2 tablespoons honey
½ cup okara
3¾ to 4 cups whole wheat
   flour
3 teaspoons baking
   powder
½ teaspoon baking soda
(¼ teaspoon salt—optional)
1 teaspoon caraway seeds
1¼ cups raisins

Nellie Twomey's Soda Bread

Here's an Irish bread that's rich, full, and delicious.

Beat the eggs slightly, add the buttermilk, honey, and okara, and mix well. Sift flour, baking powder, baking soda, and salt together and add to the egg mixture in two or three parts. Be sure to stir well after each addition of the flour.

Stir caraway seeds and raisins into the batter. The batter will be quite thick.

Preheat oven to 350°F.

Grease and flour a 10-inch frying pan or cast-iron spider. Add dough and bake for about 45 minutes, or until center springs back at a slight touch.

Yield: 1 loaf

Wheatless, Eggless, Milkless Fruit Bread

A heavy, moist bread, quite tasty and satisfying.

Preheat oven to 300°F.

The fruit should be drained as dry as possible. You can use pineapple, apricot, or peach instead of banana.

Beat the fruit, oil, honey, okara, cinnamon, vanilla, and salt together until well blended.

Mix baking soda, baking powder, and the flours into above. The dough will be quite thick.

Stir in the raisins and chopped nuts. Bake in a loaf pan for 70 to 90 minutes. The bread is done when it shrinks away from the sides of the pan.

Yield: 1 loaf

2 bananas, mashed, or
  1 cup cooked fruit
¼ cup oil
½ cup honey
1 cup okara
½ teaspoon cinnamon
1½ teaspoons vanilla
  extract
(½ teaspoon salt—optional)
½ teaspoon baking soda
2 teaspoons baking
  powder
⅔ cup rye flour
⅓ cup rice flour
½ cup raisins
½ cup chopped nuts

Pumpkin Spice Bread

Preheat oven to 350°F.

Mix the honey and dry ingredients together. In a large bowl, beat egg, pumpkin, okara, sour milk, and oil together, then add the dry ingredients and mix until well blended. Stir in nuts and fruit.

Pumpkin pie spice can be replaced by a mixture of cinnamon, ginger, nutmeg, ground allspice, and ground cloves (see page 172).

Spoon into an oiled bread pan and bake for about 1 hour. Cool for at least a half hour before removing from the pan.

Yield: 1 loaf

½ cup honey
(½ teaspoon salt—optional)
2 teaspoons pumpkin pie
  spice
1 teaspoon baking soda
2 teaspoons baking
  powder
3 cups whole wheat flour
1 egg
1 cup cooked pumpkin
½ cup okara
¼ cup sour milk or
  buttermilk
⅓ cup oil
1 to 1½ cups any
  combination of chopped
  nuts, raisins, chopped
  dates, or other dried
  fruit

Banana–Coconut–Tofu Bread (Eggless)

1 large or 2 small ripe
  bananas
½ cup tofu
½ cup oil
½ cup honey
(½ teaspoon salt—optional)
¼ cup wheat germ
2 teaspoons baking
  powder
½ teaspoon baking soda
1½ cups whole wheat
  flour
1 to 3 tablespoons soured
  milk, buttermilk, or
  yogurt
1 teaspoon vanilla extract
½ cup unsweetened
  coconut, grated or
  shredded
(½ cup chopped
  nuts—optional)
(½ cup raisins—optional)

Preheat oven to 325°F.

Mash the banana and beat with an electric mixer. Add the tofu, oil, honey, and salt. You may also use a blender at this point to get a smooth mixture, but this is not necessary.

Add the wheat germ and leavenings and about ½ cup of the flour, and beat well. Add the rest of the flour alternately with the milk or yogurt. Add the vanilla and only as much milk as necessary. The dough should be quite thick. Stir coconut, nuts, and raisins into the mixture.

Bake in an oiled 4 x 8-inch loaf pan for 1 hour or more. Check at 1 hour—the cake should be nicely browned and should have begun to pull away from the sides of the pan. If not, bake for another 10 to 20 minutes. Underbaking will make a gummy bread, and overbaking is preferable.

Yield: 1 loaf

Banana Okara Bread

¼ cup soymilk or dairy
  milk
3 mashed bananas
1 egg
½ cup butter or margarine
½ cup honey
½ cup okara
1 teaspoon baking powder
1 teaspoon baking soda
(½ teaspoon
  salt—optional)
1½ cups whole wheat
  flour
¼ cup wheat germ
(½ cup chopped
  nuts—optional)
(½ cup raisins—optional)

This easily made bread can double as a dessert.

Preheat oven to 350°F.

Cream together milk, banana, egg, butter, honey, and okara. Mix dry ingredients in a separate bowl and then add to banana mixture. Blend well, but do not beat. Add nuts and raisins if desired.

Pour the batter into a greased 5 x 9-inch pan. Bake at 350°F for about an hour.

Yield: 1 loaf

Casserole Dill Bread

This yeast bread requires no kneading and is light, savory, and fragrant. It makes the most remarkable cheese sandwiches!

Soften the yeast in the warm whey or water. In a large bowl, combine tofu, cottage cheese, honey, onion, oil, dill seed, salt, baking soda, and egg. Beat together. Add the yeast mixture and mix well.

Add wheat germ and flour, 1 cup at a time. Mix well after each addition. This will make a very stiff dough. Cover the bowl and let rise in a warm, draft-free place for about an hour.

Preheat oven to 350°F.

Stir the dough down, and place in an oiled 1½- or 2-quart casserole dish to rise again for about 40 minutes or until it is about double in size.

Bake for 40 to 50 minutes.

Yield: 1 loaf

1 tablespoon dry yeast
½ cup warm whey or water
½ cup tofu, mashed (or 1 cup, if you omit the cottage cheese)
½ cup cottage cheese
1 tablespoon honey
1 tablespoon onion, minced
1 tablespoon oil
2 teaspoons dill seed
(1 teaspoon salt—optional)
¼ teaspoon baking soda
(1 egg—optional)
¼ cup wheat germ
2¼ to 2½ cups whole wheat flour

Quick Coffee Cake

This is one of those throw-together treats that can be ready to serve in less than an hour.

Preheat oven to 350°F.

Mix the dry ingredients together, beat the wet together, and then combine the two, stirring only enough to blend.

Pour the batter into an 8 x 8-inch pan and spread evenly. (If using Topping 1, sprinkle it on). Bake for 30 minutes. Serve warm.

(continued on next page)

1½ cups any flour
3 teaspoons baking powder
(½ teaspoon salt—optional)
¼ teaspoon baking soda
½ cup okara
¼ cup wheat germ
1 egg
½ cup honey
¼ cup oil
½ cup dairy milk or buttermilk
1 teaspoon vanilla extract

½ cup honey
2 teaspoons whole wheat
    flour
2 teaspoons cinnamon
½ cup chopped nuts
2 teaspoons melted butter

TOPPING 1

Mix these ingredients together and blend well. Sprinkle over the cake batter before baking.

5 tablespoons honey
3 tablespoons melted
    butter
2 tablespoons cream
¾ cup chopped nuts

TOPPING 2 (FOR BAKED CAKE)

Mix the brown sugar and melted butter, add the cream, and blend. Stir in the nuts. Spread over a baked cake while it is still hot, put under the broiler for 3 to 5 minutes.

Scones with Okara

1½ cups whole wheat
    flour
½ teaspoon baking soda
2 teaspoons baking
    powder
(½ teaspoon
    salt—optional)
¼ pound (1 stick) butter
½ cup shortening (butter
    is best)
½ cup buttermilk or
    soured soymilk
½ cup okara
(¼ cup raisins—optional)

Serve these hot from the griddle with butter and jam or honey. Cold scones can be split and toasted.

Mix together the dry ingredients, then cut in the shortening.

Combine the buttermilk and okara and add them to the flour mixture.

Turn out on a floured surface and knead 8 or 10 times. Don't handle the dough too much, or you will develop the gluten. At this point, the raisins should be kneaded in, if desired.

Roll out the dough to ½ inch thick and cut into wedges, squares, or rounds. Bake over very low heat on an ungreased cast-iron griddle for 12 to 15 minutes on each side. Be careful not to brown the scones too much, as they should be baked through, but not fried.

Note: To sour fresh milk, mix in ½ teaspoon apple cider vinegar and let the mixture stand for 10 minutes. You will know when it is done.
Yield: 20 to 30 scones

Okara Cornsticks

These are at their best with gobs of butter.

Preheat oven to 475°F.

Oil a cast-iron muffin pan or cornstick pan with a nonburning oil, and place the pan in oven to preheat also. (Even an ordinary unheated pan will give good results, so don't hesitate to try this recipe just because you don't have the right pan.)

Mix the okara, flour, cornmeal, wheat germ, baking powder, and salt. Stir egg, milk, and oil into the dry ingredients and mix thoroughly.

Pour the mixture into the cups to about two-thirds full. Bake 12 to 14 minutes. Serve immediately.

Yield: 6 to 10 cornsticks, depending on their size

½ cup okara
¼ cup whole wheat flour
½ cup yellow cornmeal
1 tablespoon wheat germ
2 teaspoons baking powder
(½ teaspoon salt—optional)
1 egg
½ cup soymilk or dairy milk
⅓ cup oil or melted butter

Okara Bran Biscuits

Preheat oven to 350°F.

Mix the dry ingredients and work in the okara. Stir in the honey and oil and blend well. Mix in as much sour cream as is necessary to make a moist dough. Add raisins or apricots.

Drop by the tablespoonful on a baking sheet. Bake for 15 to 25 minutes, until nicely browned.

Especially nice at breakfast time, these biscuits are valuable for their high fiber content. Don't limit yourself to the suggested combination of bran, wheat germ, and flour, but try your own ratios (make sure the total equals 1¼ cups).

Yield: 16 biscuits

¼ cup bran
¼ cup wheat germ
¾ cup whole wheat flour
½ teaspoon cinnamon
½ teaspoon baking soda
1½ teaspoons baking powder
(½ teaspoon salt—optional)
½ cup okara
2 tablespoons honey
⅓ cup oil
2 to 4 tablespoons sour cream, soymilk, or yogurt
⅓ cup raisins or chopped dried apricots

Buttermilk Doughnuts

2 eggs
½ cup honey
2 tablespoons butter,
 softened
¾ cup buttermilk or
 soured soymilk
⅔ cup okara
½ cup wheat germ
3 cups whole wheat or
 other flour, mixed in
 any proportion
2 teaspoons baking
 powder
1 teaspoon baking soda
¼ teaspoon nutmeg
¼ teaspoon cinnamon
¼ teaspoon allspice

What are autumn and Halloween without doughnuts and apple cider?

Beat the eggs and mix in the honey and butter. Blend in the buttermilk and okara.

Stir the remaining ingredients into the creamed mixture, then turn onto a floured board or a pastry cloth. Roll out until the dough is ½ inch thick; let it stand for 20 minutes. Cut with a doughnut cutter or the rim of a drinking glass. If using a glass, the screw cap from a bottle will make a great cutter for the hole.

Drop into hot oil and fry until browned; drain. The holes cook faster than the doughnuts, so watch them carefully.

Yield: 10 to 20 doughnuts

Oatmeal Crackers with Tofu

1 cup rolled oats
1 cup whole wheat flour
½ cup wheat germ
(1 teaspoon salt—optional)
½ teaspoon baking soda
½ cup oil
3 to 6 tablespoons tofu,
 mashed with a fork

Mix dry ingredients. The oats can be crushed with a rolling pin to make them adhere to the dough better.

Add the oil and mix well. The dough will be rather oily, but still crumbly.

Add 3 tablespoons tofu and stir well. If the dough does not come together to form a ball, add another tablespoon. Add enough tofu to make a ball that is oily, not wet; since tofu can vary greatly in water content, add it gradually.

Knead the dough with your hands for a few seconds, smoothing it and blending the ingredients. Roll out between two sheets of wax paper. This permits you to roll the dough very thin, and yet handle it easily. Transfer to an ungreased cookie sheet, cut into squares or any shape you wish (trimming off excess dough and odd shapes for baking later). Bake at 325°F for 15 minutes or until lightly browned. Remove immediately with a spatula and cool on a wire rack.

(continued)

Work into the dough one of the following:
- ½ cup Parmesan cheese and ½ teaspoon herbs
     (oregano, parsley)
- 2 tablespoons honey, and cinnamon to taste

Sprinkle with the following prior to baking:
- onion salt or garlic salt
- caraway seeds or sesame seeds
- poppy seeds

Yield: 50   2-inch-square crackers

Tofu Okara Crackers

Tired of the high price of whole grain crackers? You will be pleased to find how simple it is to make your own.

Mix okara, flour, wheat germ, and salt.

Add oil and mix thoroughly. It should be an oily but crumbly dough.

Add the tofu gradually until the dough comes together and forms an oily ball. The amount of tofu necessary really depends upon what extra ingredients you add from the list of variations.

Preheat oven to 350°F.

Knead the dough a few seconds. Place between two sheets of wax paper and roll to ¹⁄₁₆-inch thick. Transfer the dough to a cookie sheet by peeling off the top layer of wax paper and turning a cookie sheet face down over the dough. A quick flip will transfer the bottom piece of wax paper and rolled dough to the cookie sheet. Cut the dough into the size crackers desired and trim off uneven edges to be gathered and re-rolled. Bake for 8 to 12 minutes. Cool on a wire rack.

1 cup okara
1 cup whole wheat flour
½ cup wheat germ
(1 teaspoon salt—optional)
½ cup oil
3 to 4 tablespoons tofu

(continued on next page)

125

Variations
- ⅛ cup Parmesan
  cheese and
  ⅛ teaspoon oregano
- 2 tablespoons tahini.
  Roll in sesame
  seeds by sprinkling
  seeds on wax paper
  beforehand
- 2 tablespoons peanut
  butter and
  2 teaspoons honey
- 1 tablespoon dry
  chopped onion or
  1 teaspoon onion
  powder
- ½ teaspoon garlic
  powder
- ¼ to ½ cup dry grated
  cheese
- ½ to 1 teaspoon
  mixed herbs
- ¼ to 1 teaspoon curry
  powder

Okara Flatbread

1 cup mixed flours
¼ cup gluten flour
¼ cup wheat germ or
  unprocessed bran
(¼ teaspoon
  salt—optional)
1 tablespoon oil
¾ cup okara
cold water

This easily made flatbread is great for open-face sandwiches. Serve it warm and steamed with any meal, or toast and try as a cracker for dipping.

Use any combination of flours: wheat, rye, or corn. You must include gluten flour for perfect results.

Combine the dry ingredients, and work in the oil and the okara with your fingers. Add just enough water to make a soft dough. Let the dough stand for a good half hour before using.

Knead the dough very well, the more the better. Divide it into balls about the size of a golf ball or smaller. Roll the balls very thin and bake as you would pancakes, slowly on an oiled griddle until slightly browned, but not hard. (If you have a tortilla press, this recipe will put it to good use.) Keep them warm in the oven or cool and stack for later use. They will freeze well.

Yield: 21   4- to 5-inch flatbreads

Sauces, Dips, and Spreads *12*

These customarily high-calorie, high-cholesterol preparations can be lightened with tofu, without sacrificing flavor or texture. Tofu acts as an emulsifier and stabilizer, replacing much cottage cheese, sour cream, yogurt, and ricotta.

Sauces, Dips, and Spreads
Basic White Sauce	129
Basic White Sauce from Stock (Velouté)	129
Tofu Hollandaise Sauce	131
Tofu Bearnaise Sauce	132
Ymer (with Tofu)	132
Creamy Tofu Mustard Sauce	133
Tomato Sauce	133
Sweet Yogurt Sauce	133
Fish-Flavored Sauce	134
Curry Sauce	134
Dipping Sauces for Tofu Cubes	135
Tofu Dip Base	136
Dip for Vegetables	136
Liptauer (An Austrian Dip or Spread)	137
Tofu Ghenouj	137

THE TOFU COOKBOOK

Tofu Cream Cheese 138
Cucumber Sandwich Spread 138
Seafood Spread 139
Blue Cheese Spread 139

Basic White Sauce

This recipe will make 1 cup of medium-thick white sauce. You'll find many uses for it.

Melt the butter in a heavy-bottomed saucepan. Stir in the flour and cook over low heat for 3 to 5 minutes, stirring constantly.

Remove the butter–flour mixture from the heat and add milk slowly while stirring frantically with a fork, wire whip, or slotted spoon. Cook on medium-low heat until the sauce just comes to a boil and thickens.

Yield: 1 cup

2 tablespoons butter (or oil, but it hasn't the desired flavor, and allows the soymilk to dominate)
2 tablespoons whole wheat flour
1 cup soymilk

Add one of the following for variety
- 1 tablespoon sherry wine
- ¼ teaspoon nutmeg
- ¼ teaspoon celery salt or celery seed
- 1 teaspoon lemon juice
- 1 tablespoon Worcestershire sauce
- ¼ cup chopped parsley
- ¼ to ½ teaspoon onion powder
- ¼ to ½ teaspoon garlic powder
- 2 tablespoons homemade catsup

Basic White Sauce from Stock (Velouté)

The difference between white sauce and velouté is that the latter is made with stock from meat, poultry, fish, or vegetables instead of milk or cream.

Melt the butter in a saucepan (never aluminum) and stir in the flour. Cook about 1 minute, stirring constantly, before adding stock.

2 tablespoons butter, margarine, or oil
2 tablespoons whole wheat flour
2 cups very hot stock
(continued on next page)

Suggested additions
- 1 to 2 tablespoons capers
- 2 tablespoons paprika and ½ teaspoon onion powder
- ½ cup dry white wine and ¼ teaspoon garlic powder
- 2 tablespoons dry sherry and 1 teaspoon paprika
- 2 tablespoons tomato paste
- 2 tablespoons fresh chopped herbs and 1 tablespoon vinegar
- 1 teaspoon curry powder and 1 tablespoon lemon juice

Remove the flour–butter mixture from the heat and stir in the stock, mixing and beating with a wire whip or a fork. When well blended, return to the stove and simmer until thickened.

The sauce may be used as it is, or flavored as suggested.

Yield: approximately 2 cups

PARSLEY SAUCE

¼ cup dry white wine, whey, or water
½ cup fresh parsley, chopped
pepper, to taste
1 cup Basic White Sauce

Add the wine, parsley, and pepper to the white sauce and cook for about 3 minutes. Taste and correct seasonings.

The sauce should not be cooked too long, as it will lose its fresh green color and its fresh flavor. It is excellent with broiled tofu slices and with broiled or fried fish of all kinds.

Yield: 1 ¼ cups

Tofu Hollandaise Sauce

½ cup tofu, mashed
1 tablespoon lemon juice
water to thin slightly
½ cup clarified butter

Hollandaise sauce, the classic high-cholesterol delicacy, can be made with tofu. This automatically cuts the cholesterol content in half. Although the sauce tastes best when prepared with clarified butter, it can be made with low-cholesterol margarine or with oil.

Blend the tofu, lemon juice, and water at high speed using only enough water to make blending possible. Taste, and add more lemon juice if desired.

Gradually add the butter to the above mixture while blending at high speed, and process about 1 minute.

Cook over boiling water to just below boiling; when you see the first bubble rise it is almost too late! If the sauce boils it will be ruined, as in traditional hollandaise. It will cause it to curdle.

TO RESCUE CURDLED HOLLANDAISE SAUCE

Mix 1 tablespoon whole wheat flour with about ¼ cup of the hot sauce and add this to the ruined sauce. Cook for about 1 minute. Return it to the blender and process until smooth. Serve immediately without reheating.

Since Tofu Hollandaise Sauce and the following sauces are used for garnishing, rather than drowning, hot dishes, it is not necessary for the sauce to be piping hot. In fact, it is possible to serve the sauces at room temperature. A scant tablespoon of sauce is ample for an average serving of vegetable.

Tofu Bearnaise Sauce

¼ to ½ teaspoon tarragon
   leaves
1 tablespoon onion,
   minced
5 teaspoons wine vinegar
½ cup tofu, mashed
½ teaspoon French
   Dijon-type mustard
1 tablespoon lemon juice
pepper, to taste
water to thin, if necessary
½ cup clarified butter, oil,
   or margarine

A close relative of hollandaise is bearnaise, a sauce traditionally served with red meats. Again, the sauce is at its best when made with butter, but oil or margarine will do.

Pulverize the tarragon in a mortar and combine with the onion and vinegar in a small pan. Simmer until most of the vinegar evaporates.

Blend this mixture with the tofu and flavorings at high speed, adding only enough water to make blending possible. Scrape down the sides of the bowl often.

Add the butter by droplets while blending, increasing to a steady thin stream until half the butter is added. Taste and correct seasonings. Continue adding butter until it is gone.

Place in the top of a double boiler and cook slightly to keep warm. Serve as soon as possible. If the sauce becomes too hot it will separate and can be rescued in the same way as the Tofu Hollandaise Sauce (see preceding recipe).

It is perfectly acceptable to serve both bearnaise and hollandaise sauces at room temperature or only warm. Cooking can spoil them and if you are serving the sauces on very hot food, it hardly matters that the sauce is not piping hot.

Yield: 1 cup

Ymer (with Tofu)

Make as much or as little as
you please, following these
proportions
   ⅓ yogurt
   ⅓ sour cream
   ⅓ tofu

If you can't pronounce it, you are not alone. A close approximation is "humor." What is it? A dairy concoction somewhere between sour cream and yogurt—thinner than the former, sweeter than the latter. Ymer is lower in calories than sour cream, higher than yogurt. Our version has fewer calories than either and you'll find it quite tasty as well.

Combine all ingredients in a blender and process until very smooth. Store in the refrigerator for 24 to 48 hours before using.

Ymer is used as a topping for fruit and vegetables, as a substitute for sour cream in cooking, on salads, in soups, and as a base for dips and salad dressings.

Creamy Tofu Mustard Sauce

Here is another variation of tofu sauce.

Blend tofu, lemon juice, mustard, water, and tarragon at high speed, adding water to improve the consistency. Taste and correct seasonings.

Add the oil gradually and blend for about 1 minute until smooth.

Heat over boiling water until just below boiling—any hotter and the sauce will curdle. Serve at once or set aside and serve at room temperature with vegetables.

Yield: ¾ cup

½ cup tofu
1 tablespoon lemon juice
1 teaspoon French
    Dijon-type mustard
2 to 4 tablespoons water
½ teaspoon tarragon
    leaves
¼ cup salad oil

Tomato Sauce

Serve this sauce with tofu slices, with cheese soufflé, or with omelets.

Combine all ingredients in a saucepan and simmer until the vegetables are soft. This should be a fairly thin sauce, with high flavor.

1 cup cut tomatoes,
    canned or fresh
½ cup whey
2 tablespoons onion,
    chopped
½ cup combination of
    celery, cabbage, and
    parsley, chopped
1 teaspoon lemon juice
¼ teaspoon grated lemon
    rind
1 teaspoon Worcestershire
    sauce
pepper, to taste
¼ teaspoon dry basil, or
    1 teaspoon fresh basil,
    chopped

Sweet Yogurt Sauce

Whirl all the ingredients in a blender until they are very smooth. Serve uncooked.

This sauce tastes better if allowed to mellow for a day. It can be served on crepes, pancakes, or waffles.

Yield: 1¼ cups

¾ cup yogurt
½ cup tofu
3 tablespoons honey

133

Fish-Flavored Sauce

¼ to ½ cup clam juice
¼ to ½ cup dry white
  wine
½ teaspoon onion powder
½ cup tofu, mashed
pepper, to taste
1 teaspoon cornstarch
(salt—optional)

Combine the clam juice, wine, onion powder, tofu, and pepper in the blender and process until very smooth.

Blend in the cornstarch. Heat the sauce to a simmer and stir while it thickens. If necessary, thin with water, wine, or clam juice to maintain the desired consistency. Do not allow the sauce to boil.

Serve with fish dishes, tofu slices, or spaghetti. This is a great way to get fish flavor without the fish.

Curry Sauce

3 tablespoons butter or oil
3 tablespoons whole
  wheat flour
1½ cups soymilk or whey
pepper, to taste
1 to 2 teaspoons curry
  powder, or to taste
½ teaspoon onion powder
1 teaspoon lemon juice
(1 egg yolk—optional)
(salt—optional)

This is an especially good sauce for Okara Patties (page 32).

Melt the butter or oil over low heat. Add flour to the butter and blend well; cook until thickened. Stir in the soymilk or whey.

Add the flavorings to the basic sauce and blend well. Beat in the egg yolk if a thicker, richer sauce is desired.

Serve immediately over Okara Patties or other dishes that would be complemented by the curry flavor of this sauce.

Yield: enough sauce for 4 servings

Dipping Sauces for Tofu Cubes

The small amount of tofu in each of these sauces acts as an emulsifier to keep the ingredients from separating after blending. Add more water if the sauces are too thick.

Before dinner, these sauces can be served to guests in bowls around a bowl of bite-size tofu cubes. Provide chopsticks or fondue forks. You might accompany this low-calorie appetizer with a dry white wine.

Blend until smooth. Taste and correct the seasonings.

Mustard sauce
1 tablespoon prepared
  mustard
1 teaspoon honey
2 tablespoons oil
¼ cup dry white wine
1 tablespoon tofu

Tahini sauce
1 tablespoon tahini
1 tablespoon tofu
1 tablespoon yogurt
2 tablespoons water
¼ teaspoon garlic powder
pepper, to taste

Shrimp sauce
2 tablespoons oil
1 tablespoon lemon juice
¼ teaspoon paprika
¼ cup dry white wine or
  water
¼ teaspoon garlic powder
1 tablespoon tofu
½ cup shrimp, chopped
  (stir in after blending
  other ingredients)
pepper, to taste

Wine and garlic sauce
1 tablespoon oil
1 clove garlic (blend until
  well liquified)
¼ cup red wine
1 tablespoon lemon juice
pepper, to taste
1 tablespoon tofu

Walnut sauce
2 tablespoons oil
2 tablespoons soy sauce
2 tablespoons water
1 tablespoon vinegar
1 teaspoon honey
1 teaspoon homemade
  catsup
pepper, to taste
1 tablespoon tofu
½ cup black or English
  walnuts, finely chopped
  (stir in after blending
  other ingredients)

Miso sauce
2 tablespoons miso
1 tablespoon vinegar
2 teaspoons honey
¼ cup dry white wine
pepper, to taste
1 tablespoon tofu
⅛ teaspoon powdered
  ginger

1 cup tofu, mashed
½ cup yogurt
1 tablespoon egg
    mayonnaise or Tofu
    Mayonnaise (page 105)

1 cup tofu, mashed
½ cup yogurt
½ teaspoon paprika
juice of ½ lemon
2 tablespoons chives,
    chopped
      or
¼ cup green onions,
    chopped
      or
½ teaspoon garlic, very
    finely minced (chop, do
    not press)

Tofu Dip Base

With this recipe, you can avoid the fat and cholesterol of sour cream.

Process all ingredients in a blender until very smooth. Store and use for dips, as you would sour cream.

Yield: 1 ½ cups

Dip for Vegetables

Combine the tofu, yogurt, paprika, and lemon juice in a blender and blend at high speed until smooth. Remove to a bowl and refrigerate. If the mix is too thick to blend well, add a few drops of water or skimmed milk.

For a stronger flavor, stir the onion into the above mixture before refrigerating.

Serve the dip in a glass bowl centered on a platter of fresh vegetables that might include:
    carrot sticks
    sweet pepper rounds
    scallions
    cucumber rounds or sticks
    zucchini rounds or sticks
    tomato wedges
    very thin daikon sticks
    radish roses
    cauliflower florets
    broccoli spears
    lettuce leaves
    mushroom slices

Liptauer (An Austrian Dip or Spread)

This is a free adaptation of an Austrian dish that is served in restaurants as little heaps of the separate ingredients. The patron then mixes the spread himself, to his own taste. (Of course the original recipe does not call for tofu.)

Put the tofu in a blender. Add the butter in a stream through the cap while blending at a fairly high speed. Blend until smooth, pour into a bowl and refrigerate until the mixture becomes firm.

Stir all the remaining ingredients except the paprika into the tofu–butter mixture and blend well.

Stir in only enough paprika to make the dip a light pink. It tastes best when it is allowed to set for several hours or overnight.

Serve the Liptauer with crackers, celery sticks, and radishes. Be sure to set the dip out to soften before serving.

Yield: 1 ½ cups

1 cup tofu, mashed
½ cup melted butter
1 teaspoon French
    Dijon-type mustard
1 teaspoon onion,
    chopped
1 or 2 anchovies, mashed
1 teaspoon parsley,
    chopped
1 teaspoon chives (or
    additional onion),
    chopped
1 teaspoon capers,
    chopped
pepper, to taste
½ teaspoon paprika

Tofu Ghenouj

Here is an adaptation of a famous old Persian dip made with eggplant. Without the eggplant, this dip is a great deal easier to make.

The tofu should be fairly dry. Process all ingredients in a blender at high speed until they are smooth and creamy. If the mixture is too thick, add a few drops of soymilk or dairy milk. If too thin, add a bit more tofu.

Serve with steamed pocket bread, cut in small wedges. This is a very impressive appetizer.

Yield: approximately 2 cups

1 cup tofu, pressed
¼ cup tahini
½ cup yogurt
½ teaspoon garlic powder
(salt—optional)

Tofu Cream Cheese

3 ounces cream cheese
⅓ cup tofu, mashed and
  drained
1 to 2 tablespoons yogurt
  or sour cream

*If you wish, chop up one
  or more of the
  following for extra
  flavor*
¼ cup any nuts
⅓ cup black olives
1 tablespoon chives
1 tablespoon pimento
jalapeño peppers, to
  taste
1 to 3 tablespoons
  ham

By cutting the amount of cream cheese in half, you save calories, cholesterol, and money.

Soften the cream cheese with a fork or by allowing it to warm outside of the refrigerator. Blend in the tofu and yogurt or sour cream as necessary. This will probably be too thick for a blender, but you can try. A beater will do well.

Refrigerate for a day or so before using. The flavor will improve considerably.

Yield: 1 cup

Cucumber Sandwich Spread

⅓ cup tofu, mashed
2 tablespoons egg
  mayonnaise or Tofu
  Mayonnaise (page 105)
1 tablespoon scallion,leek,
  or onion, finely chopped
pepper, to taste
¾ to 1 cup cucumber,
  finely chopped

Place the tofu in a bowl, mix in the mayonnaise and flavorings. Taste and correct the seasonings. Mix in the cucumber. Chill and serve with toast or crackers.

Yield: 2 to 4 servings

Seafood Spread

Chop, shred, or mash the fish. Sprinkle the lemon juice over it and mix with the pepper.

Blend the tofu with the mayonnaise and sour cream until very smooth. Use drops of buttermilk to thin, if necessary.

Mix the tofu with the fish mixture and chill. Serve on bread with lettuce leaves or tomatoes.

1 cup cooked fish or
   shrimp
1 teaspoon lemon juice
pepper, to taste
½ to 1 cup tofu
1 tablespoon egg
   mayonnaise or Tofu
   Mayonnaise (page 105)
¼ cup sour cream
drops of buttermilk

Blue Cheese Spread

Mash together the blue cheese and butter or margarine and mix in the seasonings.

Process tofu and buttermilk in a blender until very smooth, adding just enough milk or yogurt to make blending possible.

Stir the tofu and blue cheese mixture together. Refrigerate and serve a day or so later; the spread improves with age and keeps for 1 or 2 weeks. Serve with celery sticks, carrot sticks, green onions, or crackers. This spread is especially good on thinly sliced pumpernickel.

¼ pound blue cheese
2 tablespoons butter or
   margarine, softened
¼ teaspoon garlic powder
½ cup tofu
drops of buttermilk or
   yogurt

139

13 Breakfasts

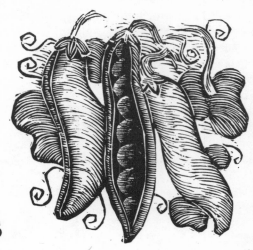

These recipes show how soyfoods work in traditional breakfasts.

Breakfasts
- Klondike Pancakes 141
- Persian Pancakes 141
- Æbleskiver (Spherical Danish Pancakes) 142
- Okara Sourdough Pancakes and Waffles 143
- Dieter's Pancakes 144
- Okara Whole Wheat Waffles 144
- Rice Flour–Okara Waffles 145
- Scrambled Tofu (with or without Eggs) 145
- Cornmeal Cereal 146
- French Toast 147
- Risengrød (Rice Cooked in Milk) 147
- Okara Sausage Patties 148

Klondike Pancakes

These yeast pancakes are low in sodium; make them without salt for people on sodium-restricted diets. Try them and you may never make baking-powder-and-soda pancakes again.

Scald the milk, add shortening, stir in the honey and okara, and cool to lukewarm.

Dissolve the yeast in the warm water, and stir into the cooled milk mixture.

Beat the tofu into the mixture, then blend in the flour and wheat germ. The batter should be fairly thick. If it is not, add more flour; if it is too thick, add a bit more milk.

Cover the bowl and let the batter stand in a warm, draft-free place for about an hour or until double in bulk. Bake on a lightly oiled griddle using about ¼ cup of batter for each cake. Stir the batter down before each batch is baked. Serve with butter or margarine, and syrup.

1 cup scalded soymilk or
   dairy milk
¼ cup shortening
2 tablespoons honey
½ cup okara
1 tablespoon dry yeast
¼ cup warm water
¼ cup tofu, mashed
1 cup whole wheat flour
   (or half whole wheat
   and half rye flour)
¼ cup wheat germ

WAFFLE VARIATION

Add ¼ cup more oil and enough extra flour to bring the dough to the right consistency for your waffle tastes. That's all! If the dough is too thick, stir in more soymilk, whey, or water.
Yield: 16   4-inch pancakes

Persian Pancakes

Mix the dry ingredients together, then add the okara and blend well.

Combine the honey, oil, and buttermilk and add them to the dry ingredients. Stir only until the mixture is blended, do not beat.

The dough for these pancakes should be as thin as that for crepes, and the pancakes should cook up with holes in them and be quite crisp. Stack the pancakes and set them aside, or fill them as you make them with the filling below.

Serve with a honey syrup and sprinkles of shredded coconut.
Yield: 20 to 30 pancakes

½ cup whole wheat pastry
   flour
½ teaspoon baking
   powder
1 teaspoon baking soda
1 cup buckwheat flour
¼ cup dry okara
2 teaspoons honey
2 tablespoons oil
3 cups buttermilk or
   soured soymilk

(continued on next page)

1 cup tofu, mashed, or
   ½ cup tofu and ½ cup
   dry cottage cheese
¼ cup honey
1 teaspoon cinnamon
¼ cup raisins
(1 egg—optional)

1 teaspoon cornstarch
1 tablespoon cold water
½ cup honey
½ cup hot water

FILLING

This filling can also be used for blintzes.

Combine all ingredients and blend well. To fill, place 1 large teaspoonful of the filling into each pancake and roll. Fit them tightly into an oiled baking dish and bake at 350°F for 10 minutes.

HONEY SYRUP

Dissolve cornstarch in cold water. Stir in with honey and hot water.

Cook until thickened.

Æbleskiver (Spherical Danish Pancakes)

3 eggs, separated
2 cups buttermilk
½ cup okara
2 tablespoons oil
½ teaspoon baking soda
1 teaspoon baking powder
2 cups whole wheat pastry
   flour
¼ cup wheat germ

Æbleskiver translates to "apple slices" but this recipe doesn't call for them. Baking these properly calls for a special iron pan, but if you don't have one, an ordinary griddle will do fine.

Separate the eggs and place the whites in a bowl. Beat the whites until stiff.

In a large bowl, beat well the egg yolks, buttermilk, okara, oil, baking soda, and baking powder.

Add flour and wheat germ and stir until thoroughly combined. Carefully fold in the egg white.

An æbleskiver pan should be used over high heat. Put 1 teaspoon oil into each hole. Fill about three-quarters full with the batter and cook until the edges begin to turn golden brown. Adjust the heat to prevent burning. When they are nicely browned, turn them and brown the other side (a knitting needle is a very handy tool for turning the cakes).

If you are using a griddle, you do not have to use 1 teaspoon of oil for each cake, but oil is necessary to make them crispy.

Serve piping hot with jam, jelly, applesauce, honey, or any other favorite topping.

Yield: 4 to 6 servings

142

Okara Sourdough Pancakes and Waffles

Remove the sourdough starter (see recipe on page 116) from the refrigerator and pour 1½ cups into a large mixing bowl. Add flour and whey and stir well. Cover and let stand overnight at room temperature. Be sure to use a bowl that is large enough to allow for lots of rising or you will find your counter covered with dough in the morning. If you wish a very sour flavor, place the basic batter in the refrigerator the next morning and plan to use it within a few days.

Stir the sourdough batter well and remove 1½ cups to your refrigerator sourdough container.

The number of eggs is up to you. The more eggs the richer, of course, but delicious pancakes and waffles can be made with just one egg (or use no eggs, and add ¼ cup tofu). Separate the eggs and add yolks to the batter.

Add honey, butter, okara, and baking soda (if desired), and mix well. If the dough is thinner than you wish, add up to 1 cup of additional flour, ¼ cup at a time. Be sure to stir well after each addition.

If the dough is too thick, thin slightly with soymilk or dairy milk.

Add optional ingredients at this point if desired. Then beat the egg whites until stiff, and gently fold them into the mixture.

The sourdough starter you have made and used in this recipe can be used in breads, muffins, rolls, and biscuits, and offers a wonderful way to cut down or eliminate sodium products from raised baked goods.

Yield: about 24 pancakes

BASIC BATTER

1½ cups sourdough
  starter
2½ cups whole wheat
  flour
3 cups warm whey or
  water

BASIC PANCAKE AND WAFFLE BATTER

1 to 4 eggs, separated, or
  ¼ cup tofu
1 tablespoon honey
2 tablespoons butter,
  melted for pancakes, ⅓
  cup for waffles
1 cup okara
(½ teaspoon baking soda,
  to remove sour
  taste—optional)
whole wheat flour or
  soymilk, as needed

Suggested variations
  • ½ to 1 cup chopped
    nuts
  • ½ cup wheat germ
  • ¼ to ½ cup
    unprocessed bran
  • ¼ cup yellow
    cornmeal

Dieter's Pancakes √√

3 eggs
½ cup cottage cheese
1 cup tofu
3 tablespoons whole
    wheat flour
2 tablespoons wheat germ
½ teaspoon baking soda
¼ cup water or whey
    (more water is needed
    with dry tofu)
1 tablespoon oil, for frying

These high-protein, low-calorie pancakes are remarkably light—a dieter can feel virtuous. Each pancake (of 2 tablespoons batter) has about 37 calories including the oil in which they are cooked. Each pancake has a whopping 2¼ grams of high-grade protein. Of course, the whole matter lies in what you put on top.

Combine all ingredients in a blender and process until smooth. Check consistency and add more water or whey if necessary. The consistency should be like whipped cream.

Pour the oil into a dish and use a piece of paper towel to apply it to the griddle. Since there is no shortening in these pancakes, the oil on the griddle is essential; without it, they will stick and you won't be able to turn them. Cook over medium heat until bubbles rise, then turn.

Yield: 24   3½-inch pancakes

Okara Whole Wheat Waffles

2 eggs
2½ cups soymilk or dairy
    milk
⅓ cup oil
1½ cups okara
2 cups whole wheat flour
¼ cup wheat germ
¼ teaspoon baking soda
1½ teaspoons baking
    powder

These waffles are fine for breakfast with the traditional syrup and butter topping, but you might also try fresh fruit, applesauce, or preserved fruits.

Separate the eggs and beat the whites until they are stiff but not dry. Set the whites aside and beat the yolks in a large bowl.

Add the soymilk, oil, and okara to the egg yolks and beat well.

Add in the remaining ingredients a little at a time and mix well after each addition. Do not overbeat. Fold in the beaten egg whites and bake at once on a preheated waffle iron.

Rice Flour–Okara Waffles

These are wonderfully crisp and satisfying. You'll find them a welcome change of pace from ordinary waffles.

Sift together the flour, baking powder, and baking soda. Beat the egg yolks and add the butter, soymilk, and okara. Beat in the flour mixture gradually.

Beat the egg whites until stiff and gently fold them into the batter. Bake on a preheated waffle iron. Serve with syrup mixed with whey, honey, or preserves.

1¾ cups rice flour
3 teaspoons baking powder
¼ teaspoon baking soda
2 eggs, separated
3 tablespoons melted butter or margarine
1½ cups soymilk or dairy milk
½ cup okara

Scrambled Tofu (with or without Eggs)

The first version will please egg lovers, while cutting down on cholesterol. The second may not take the place of scrambled eggs, but give it a try.

(continued on next page)

145

SCRAMBLED EGG WITH TOFU ✓

1 egg
1 tablespoon yogurt
¼ cup tofu, mashed
½ teaspoon butter
½ teaspoon oil

Blend together the egg, yogurt, and tofu with either a blender or an electric mixer. Fry in the melted butter and oil until dry.
Yield: 1 serving

SCRAMBLED TOFU

½ cup tofu, mashed
2 tablespoons yogurt
1 teaspoon oil or melted butter
½ teaspoon dehydrated onion
1 teaspoon butter
1 teaspoon oil

Blend together the tofu, yogurt, oil or butter, and onion and fry in the butter and oil mixture only until hot.
Yield: 1 serving

Cornmeal Cereal

¾ cup white or yellow cornmeal
⅓ cup cold water
3 cups boiling water or whey
1 cup wet okara

Cereal lovers who love cornmeal mush but aren't wild about the calories can use okara up to half-and-half without any loss of flavor or texture.

Stir together the cornmeal and water. Gradually stir the cornmeal mixture into the boiling water, and slowly add the okara. Cook until it reaches the desired consistency.

The flavor will improve if the mush is cooked in a double boiler and allowed to stand over hot water for up to an hour before serving. It can, however, be served immediately.

Press leftover corn cereal into a loaf pan and refrigerate. It can then be sliced and fried. Serve either for breakfast or for dinner with a gravy.
Yield: 4 servings

French Toast

French toast without eggs sounds impossible, but try these recipes.

For either recipe, process all ingredients in a blender until very smooth. Soak slices of your favorite bread in the mixture, and fry in butter and oil.

Serve with honey, syrup, or jam.

RECIPE 1

½ cup tofu, mashed
¼ cup yogurt
½ cup soymilk or dairy milk
1 tablespoon cornstarch
pinch of nutmeg or cinnamon
butter and oil for frying

RECIPE 2

½ cup tofu, mashed
2 tablespoons yogurt
½ cup soymilk or dairy milk
1 teaspoon oil
1 tablespoon whole wheat flour
pinch of cinnamon or nutmeg
1 teaspoon vanilla extract
1 teaspoon honey
butter and oil, for frying

Risengrød (Rice Cooked in Milk)

This is an adaptation of a traditional Danish dish. Adding okara to the cereal cuts both the gumminess and the calories.

Wash the rice and add okara and soymilk. Cook over water for at least an hour (even overnight).

It will be necessary to add milk or water to the cooking rice from time to time. When fully cooked the risengrød should be just a bit thicker than other hot cereals.

1 cup white pearl rice
1 cup okara
2 cups soymilk or dairy milk

(continued on next page)

Serve the risengrød on a flat plate with a large pat of butter in the center and a shaker of cinnamon and honey. This can be served as a cereal, or as a whole evening meal. Save the leftovers for a delicious dessert, made by mixing it with whipped cream and slivered almonds. Serve with a dab of preserves in the center.
Yield: 4 servings

Okara Sausage Patties

1 cup okara
¼ cup powdered milk
1 egg

Pick one of the following
- 1 cup potatoes, mashed
- 1 cup any cooked cereal
- 1 cup sausage and cereal or mashed potatoes, in any proportion
- 2 slices nitrite-free bacon, chopped very fine, and any of the above to equal 1 cup

⅛ to ¼ teaspoon sage
⅛ to ¼ teaspoon summer savory
⅛ to ¼ teaspoon thyme
⅛ to ¼ teaspoon nutmeg
⅛ to ¼ teaspoon paprika
⅛ to ¼ teaspoon ground anise
pepper, to taste
oil, for frying

If you like pork sausage for breakfast, but are put off by the cholesterol, the sodium, and the calories, try this recipe.

Combine the okara, powdered milk, and egg. Add your choice of the potato, cereal, sausage, or bacon, and mix well. Add the spices and mix well again, using either an electric mixer or your hands.

Form the sausage into patties and fry in oil over a medium heat until very crisp and nicely browned. Drain and keep in a warm oven until serving time.
Yield: 4 servings

Desserts: Pies, Cakes, Cookies, and Assorted Fancies 14

Tofu may seem an unlikely ingredient in desserts. But you'll find that it creates an impression of richness without loading on calories or cholesterol.

Desserts: Pies, Cakes, Cookies, and Assorted Fancies
Tofu Cheese Pie	150
Yogurt Pie (Yiaourtopeta)	151
Eggless Lemon Pie	151
Sweet Pie Shell	152
Tofu Cheese Torte	152
Hazelnut Okara Torte	153
Basic Soy Custard (Baked)	153
Eggnog Mousse (Bavarian Cream)	154
Spanish Creme	155
Basic Mousse	155
Fudge Brownies	156
Oatmeal Okara Cookies	156
Okara and Coconut Macaroons	157
Zucchini Cookies	157
Okara Tofu Spice Bars (Eggless)	158
Fruit Dumplings	159
Okara Carrot Cake	159
Okara Blueberry Cake	160

Tofu Cheese Pie

2 tablespoons cornstarch
¼ cup cold water
2 eggs
½ cup honey
2 teaspoons vanilla extract
1 cup tofu
1 cup creamed cottage
  cheese
¼ teaspoon grated lemon
  rind
2 teaspoons lemon juice
⅓ cup melted butter or
  margarine (not oil)

Preheat oven to 350°F.

Put the cornstarch and water in a blender and process until smooth.

Add the remaining ingredients and blend until very smooth.

Pour into a prepared Sweet Pie Shell (page 152) and bake at 350°F for 30 to 40 minutes. The center may still be a bit soft. It is important to avoid overcooking. An inserted silver knife should *not* come out entirely clean. Remove and cool for about 5 minutes before adding the topping. (If you don't use the topping, cool and then refrigerate.)

TOPPING

1 cup sour cream or sour
  half-and-half
1 to 2 tablespoons honey,
  or to taste
(1 teaspoon vanilla
  extract—optional)

Stir together all the ingredients and pour over the top of the slightly cooled pie. Return to a 350°F oven for no more than 5 minutes. Cool and refrigerate before serving.
Yield: 8 to 10 servings

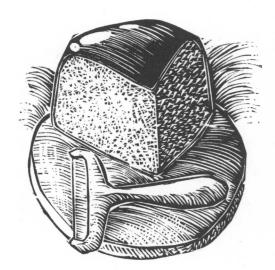

Yogurt Pie (Yiaourtopeta)

This is an adaptation of a very simple and delicious uncooked dessert.

Place tofu, yogurt, cream cheese, vanilla, and honey in a blender and process at high speed until it is very smooth.

Plump the raisins in boiling water and dry well on a paper towel. Stir into the above mixture. (Do not blend.)

Pour the mixture into the cooled prebaked pie shell and refrigerate for at least a day before serving.

½ pound (1¼ cups) fresh tofu
1 cup yogurt
3 ounces cream cheese
1 teaspoon vanilla extract
¼ cup honey
(½ cup white or dark raisins—optional)
1 baked Sweet Pie Shell (page 152)

Eggless Lemon Pie

A light, velvety, refreshing pie.

Mix the honey and cornstarch together and add the water. Cook stirring continuously until thickened.

Blend tofu, lemon juice, and lemon rind until smooth, then gradually add the hot mixture and blend well. Return this mixture to the pan and cook for a short time, until very hot but not boiling. If you boil the filling by accident, return it to the blender and process until smooth again, but do not reheat.

Pour into a baked 10-inch pie shell and refrigerate until cool. For a richer pie, cool the mixture before putting it into the shell and fold in 1 cup of whipped cream; or fold whipped cream in the custard and top with whipped cream as well. It is all a matter of calories.

You can adapt this basic eggless pie recipe by using milk instead of lemon juice and flavoring it with vanilla. Fold in bananas or coconut or what you will.

Yield: 6 to 8 servings

⅔ cup honey
¼ to ⅓ cup cornstarch
2 cups water or whey
1 cup tofu
½ cup lemon juice, or to taste
2 teaspoons grated lemon rind
1 prebaked pie shell

Sweet Pie Shell

1 cup bread crumbs
½ cup dry okara
4–5 teaspoons honey
(½ teaspoon
    cinnamon—optional)
2 tablespoons melted
    butter

Preheat oven to 325°F.

This pie shell is suitable for all cream-type pies, for lemon pie, for pudding pies, and for unbaked fruit pies. It is prebaked and used for fillings only.

Any kind of bread crumbs will do except perhaps bread with caraway seeds. If you use sweet crumbs, from leftover cake or cookies, adjust the honey accordingly.

Combine crumbs, okara, honey, and cinnamon in a blender, pouring in the melted butter.

Put into a 9- or 10-inch pie pan with your fingers or a fork, piling the crust well up on the sides of the pan. Bake at 325°F for 10 to 20 minutes. Cool before using.

Tofu Cheese Torte

1 baked Sweet Pie Shell
    (page 152)
½ cup oil
1⅛ cups honey
6 tablespoons cornstarch
2 tablespoons whole
    wheat flour
6 cups (1½ pounds) dry
    cottage cheese
3 cups tofu
8 large eggs
3 teaspoons vanilla extract
2 cups yogurt
½ teaspoon cinnamon
(1 cup raisins—optional)

Use 1½ times the recipe for one Sweet Pie Shell, and bake it in a springform pan. If you do not have a springform pan, use a deep cake pan or pie pan.

Preheat the oven to 325°F.

Combine oil, honey, cornstarch, flour, cottage cheese, and tofu in a blender and process until very smooth; if necessary, separate into two batches to blend properly. Pour into a large bowl.

Blend eggs, vanilla, yogurt, and cinnamon at medium speed. Add 1 or 2 cups of the tofu mixture and mix again. Pour into a bowl with the cheese mixture and beat together well.

Pour the filling into the crust-lined springform pan, add raisins, pushing them down with a spoon, and bake for 1½ hours or until the torte puffs up and holds its shape. When cool, refrigerate.

(The texture depends on how firm the tofu is, since some contain more liquid than others. You can allow excess liquid to drain from the tofu for about a half hour before using.)
Yield: 12 to 14 servings

Hazelnut Okara Torte

This is a rich dessert, containing a lot of eggs and honey.

Oil and flour 2 layer-cake tins. Preheat the oven to 325°F.

Separate the eggs and set the yolks aside. Beat the whites until foamy, sprinkle in the cream of tartar, and beat until stiff.

Very gradually add 3 tablespoons of the honey to the egg whites, beating continuously.

In a separate bowl, beat the egg yolks until they are light and foamy, and gradually add the rest of the honey.

Add the okara to the yolk mixture a tablespoon at a time, beating after each addition. Gradually add the nuts.

Carefully fold the egg whites into the yolk mixture, retaining as many air bubbles as possible.

Bake for 20 minutes or more; the torte should spring back when touched and should be a light brown. Cool on a rack before removing from the pans. Serve the torte with whipped cream. Carob-flavored whipped cream is especially good.

6 eggs, separated
¼ teaspoon cream of tartar
⅓ cup honey
½ cup okara
1 cup hazelnuts (filberts), chopped fine

Basic Soy Custard (Baked)

Custards are based on a judicious mixture of eggs and milk, often with the addition of a sweetener. The basis of a good quiche is custard, and it is the essence of a Crème Renversée as well. The difference is in the amount of sweetening, flavoring, and egg yolk used. An ordinary light custard includes 1 egg yolk to each cup of milk. A richer custard will have many egg yolks and not so many egg whites. For instance, a 5-egg yolk dessert will make you swoon while a 1-egg yolk custard will remind you of childhood illnesses. It is all a matter of cholesterol.

Melt the butter in hot soymilk. Beat the eggs until foamy. Gradually add the honey. While beating, add the hot milk in a thin stream. Add the vanilla.

Pour the mixture into a buttered baking dish or into small individual molds. Place in a shallow pan of water and bake at 325°F for 35 to 45 minutes or until a knife inserted into the middle comes out clean. Cool before serving.

Yield: 2 ½ cups

1 tablespoon butter
2 cups soymilk, scalded
2 whole eggs
¼ cup honey
¼ teaspoon vanilla extract

(continued on next page)

VARIATIONS

With 2 cups of milk you may use up to 6 egg yolks, ¼ cup honey, and perhaps 3 or 4 whites. The more yolks, the richer the custard. Reserve the excess whites for use in soufflés, tortes, and confections. Egg whites freeze well and can be kept indefinitely.
Yield: 3⅓ cups

Eggnog Mousse (Bavarian Cream)

(1 or 2 eggs—optional)
1 cup tofu
1 cup soymilk or dairy milk
¼ cup honey
½ teaspoon freshly ground nutmeg
1 teaspoon unflavored gelatin
2 tablespoons cold water
1 to 2 tablespoons whiskey or brandy
1 teaspoon vanilla extract
(1 cup whipped cream—optional)

Blend eggs, tofu, milk, honey, and nutmeg. Pour in a heavy-bottomed saucepan and bring nearly to a boil, stirring constantly. (The eggs add richness and flavor, but are unnecessary.)

Soften gelatin in cold water. Add to the hot mixture and stir well. Remove from heat and stir in whiskey or brandy and vanilla.

Return the mixture to the blender and blend for a few seconds until smooth. Chill in a bowl in the refrigerator.

When the pudding is cooled and set, whip until foamy with an electric beater and fold in the whipped cream.

Spoon the mixture into a mold or into individual serving dishes and chill. Serve plain or with a fruit sauce such as the one below.
Yield: 4 servings

APRICOT HARD SAUCE

1 cup apricot preserves (berry preserves can be used)
¼ cup water
1 teaspoon rum, or flavored liqueur such as curaçao, Mirabelle, or Cointreau

Stir preserves and water together and heat. Remove from heat and stir in flavoring. Serve hot or cold with eggnog mousse or your favorite pudding.

Spanish Creme

A light and refreshing dessert.

Soften the gelatin in ¼ cup of the cold soymilk. In the top of a double boiler mix the egg yolks and honey, blending well. Add the remaining soymilk. Cook until the mixture coats a spoon, but do not boil. Stir in the honey and gelatin until they are completely dissolved. Cool until the mixture is completely set.

Beat the egg whites and fold in the vanilla. Refrigerate again until set. Serve plain or with a teaspoon of red jelly, such as currant.

Yield: 6 servings

1 tablespoon unflavored
  gelatin
2 cups cold soymilk
2 eggs, separated
⅓ cup honey
1 teaspoon vanilla extract

Basic Mousse

Soften the gelatin in the cold water. Stir together the soymilk and honey and bring to a boil. Add the gelatin mixture and stir until the gelatin is dissolved. Cool.

Add vanilla to the cooled mixture. Combine the above mixture and the tofu in a blender and process at high speed until very smooth.

Cool the mixture in the refrigerator until almost set. Remove, and beat by hand or with an electric mixer until light and fluffy. Freeze the mixture in a mold or in a refrigerator tray for about 1 to 2 hours, depending on the size of the mold. Serve before it becomes too hard.

Yield: 6 to 8 servings

2 teaspoons unflavored
  gelatin
1 cup cold water
1 cup soymilk
1 cup honey
2 teaspoons vanilla extract
2 cups tofu, mashed

Variations
- ½ to 1 cup frozen fruit
  (if sweetened,
  reduce honey to
  taste)
- 2 tablespoons carob
  powder and
  2 tablespoons
  instant coffee
- 2 tablespoons carob
  powder
- ½ to 1 cup fruit
  preserves
- spices, raisins, and
  nuts

Fudge Brownies

3 tablespoons butter
½ cup honey
2 eggs
¼ cup okara
1 teaspoon vanilla extract
¼ teaspoon baking soda
6 tablespoons carob
    powder
3 teaspoons oil, or melted
    butter or margarine
⅓ cup whole wheat flour
1 tablespoon wheat germ
1 cup chopped nuts

Preheat oven to 325°F.

Cream the butter and gradually add the honey. Add eggs, okara, vanilla, and baking soda and beat well.

In a separate bowl, thoroughly mix carob, oil, flour, and wheat germ. Add to the above mixture. Stir in the chopped nuts.

Pour the batter into an oiled, shallow 8 x 13-inch pan and spread evenly. Bake for 30 minutes.

If undercooked, these brownies will have a more fudgelike quality; if cooked too long or too hot, they will be hard and dry.

Oatmeal Okara Cookies

½ cup butter, softened
½ cup honey
1 egg
½ teaspoon baking soda
1 teaspoon vanilla extract
1 cup whole wheat flour
1½ cups oatmeal
½ cup dry okara
½ cup raisins
½ cup walnuts, chopped

Variations
Replace the oatmeal with
    either of the following:
- 1½ cups granola
- 1½ cups mixed oats,
    granola, wheat
    germ, and bran

You'll find these sweet and delicious.

Preheat oven to 350°F.

Combine the softened butter and honey. Beat in the egg and blend well.

Add baking soda and vanilla, and mix thoroughly.

Beat in the flour, then stir in the remaining ingredients.

Drop by teaspoonsful on an oiled cookie sheet. Bake for 10 to 12 minutes. Remove from the cookie sheet as soon as you take them out of the oven and cool on racks or, better yet, a brown paper bag, open and laid flat on the counter or table.

Yield: 35   3-inch cookies

Okara and Coconut Macaroons

Preheat oven to 350°F.

Mix ingredients together well. Grease and flour a baking sheet. Drop the mixture by tablespoonsful on the sheet and bake for about 10 minutes or until lightly toasted. Place on waxed paper immediately after you remove them from the oven.

Yield: 3 dozen

½ cup condensed milk
2 tablespoons honey
2 cups coconut, shredded
   or grated
½ cup okara
¼ cup wheat germ
1 teaspoon vanilla extract

Zucchini Cookies

This may come to be a real favorite, as well as being a unique method of using zucchini. The recipe is also a good way to get children to eat this vegetable.

Preheat oven to 375°F.

Beat together butter and honey until smooth. Stir in remaining ingredients, and refrigerate dough until stiff and manageable.

Drop by teaspoonsful onto an ungreased cookie sheet, flatten, and bake for 10 to 12 minutes.

Yield: 4 to 5 dozen

½ cup butter
¾ cup honey
1 egg
2 teaspoons grated lemon
   or orange rind
1½ cups whole wheat
   flour
½ cup wheat germ
½ cup okara
1 cup whole wheat flour
1 teaspoon baking powder
1 teaspoon vanilla extract
1½ cups zucchini,
   shredded, drained onto
   paper towels

Okara Tofu Spice Bars (Eggless)

⅓ cup okara
½ cup tofu
⅓ cup oil
¾ cup honey
1 cup pumpkin pulp or applesauce
½ cup buttermilk or soured soymilk
2 teaspoons pumpkin pie spice
1 teaspoon baking soda
2 teaspoons baking powder
¼ cup wheat germ or unprocessed bran
2½ cups whole wheat or mixed flour
raisins, chopped dried fruit, and nuts, as desired

These bars have a very moist texture and a fine flavor. The lack of egg makes them less cakey. They are delicious served for dessert with whipped cream or ice cream topping.

Preheat oven to 325°F.

Combine okara, tofu, oil, honey, pumpkin or applesauce, and buttermilk in a blender and mix at high speed. If the mixture is too thick, add a little more buttermilk or soymilk.

Combine dry ingredients and add them to the okara mixture. The batter will be quite thick and rather sticky. Add fruit and nuts and stir until they are distributed evenly.

Spoon batter into an 8½ x 10½-inch baking pan and spread it evenly. Bake for 35 to 45 minutes or until the top springs back to the touch.

Fruit Dumplings

This quick and easy dessert can be served hot from the stove, with hard sauce, heavy cream, or just plain.

Combine fruit, water, and honey in a 2-quart saucepan. Bring to a boil, cover, and simmer over a low heat while preparing the dough. You may need the water if the fruit is dry.

Mix the flour, okara, honey, and dry ingredients together. Cut butter into the dry mixture until it is well blended and resembles coarse meal.

Stir in the buttermilk until the dough is just moist. Drop the batter on top of the simmering fruit with a spoon. Cover the pan and continue to simmer for 15 minutes. (Don't peek!) Cool slightly but serve while still quite warm.

Yield: 4 to 6 servings

2 cups fresh or frozen fruit: raspberries, blueberries, apples, or pineapple
½ cup water (if necessary)
½ cup honey
1 cup whole wheat flour
½ cup okara
3 tablespoons honey
½ teaspoon baking soda
1 teaspoon baking powder
¼ to ½ teaspoon ground cardamom
½ cup butter
2 tablespoons buttermilk or soured soymilk

Okara Carrot Cake

This is a moist cake.

Preheat oven to 350°F.

Combine the dry ingredients (sifting is not necessary). Set aside. Beat eggs and add okara in a large bowl. Gradually add the honey to the egg–okara mixture and beat well.

Alternately add the oil and dry ingredients to the batter. Mix well, but do not beat.

Fold in the raisins, nuts, and carrots and pour into an oiled 9 x 9-inch pan. Bake for 30 to 40 minutes.

1 cup whole wheat or mixed flour
¼ cup wheat germ
1 teaspoon baking soda
1 teaspoon baking powder
1 teaspoon cinnamon
2 eggs
½ cup okara
½ cup honey
¾ cup oil
½ cup raisins
½ cup any nuts, chopped
1 cup carrots, grated

Okara Blueberry Cake

1 pound blueberries
¼ pound butter, softened
½ cup honey
2 eggs, separated
¼ cup soymilk or dairy
   milk
½ cup okara
½ teaspoon cinnamon
½ teaspoon nutmeg
1 teaspoon baking powder
¼ teaspoon baking soda
1¼ cups whole wheat
   flour

Try serving with a little cream cheese on the side.

Preheat oven to 350°F.

Wash and drain the blueberries, sprinkle them lightly with flour. Combine the butter and the honey. Add the egg yolks and milk; stir in the okara.

Mix the dry ingredients together and add them to the batter. The dough will be very thick.

Beat the egg whites until they are stiff and then fold them in gently. Add the berries last.

Bake in an oiled 8 x 12-inch pan 25 to 35 minutes or until springy.

Kids' Specials and Baby Food   15

Kids tend to be picky eaters, in part because they are the object of so much junk-food advertising. They may well push the plate away the first time you bring tofu to the table.

The next several recipes are straightforward enough so that children can do most of the cooking. Through participation, they should come to like this strange new food.

Use your own judgement as to whether or not your kids should use the stove, handle hot ingredients, or operate the blender.

In baby food recipes, tofu lends protein in an easily digestible form.

Kids' Specials and Baby Food
Glorious Mess	163
Fantastic Island Soup	163
Tofu Toybox	164
Ms. Muffett Soup	165
Whey Soup	165
Carrot and Tofu Salad	165
Red, White, and Brown Rounds	165
Tofu Smoothie	166

THE TOFU COOKBOOK

Soy Shake 166
Coconut Mothballs 166
Old Cake Cookies 167
Frisbee® Cookies 167
Michelle's Mud Pies 168
Baby Cereal 168
Baby Stew or Soup 169
Baby Vegetable 169
Baby Fruit 170

Glorious Mess

This recipe is good fun, even though the results do look something like an inside-out taco.

Sauté the tofu and onion in the oil until the onions are clear.

Add the remaining ingredients and simmer for 10 minutes.

Spoon out and serve over a bed of corn chips or brown rice. Top with a salad of lettuce, chopped tomatoes, onion, and pepper, plus your favorite dressing.

Yield: 4 servings

1 pound tofu, cubed
1 onion, chopped
1 tablespoon oil
4 tomatoes, wedged
1½ cups cooked pinto beans
1 cup cooked kidney beans
½ cup whey or water
1 teaspoon powdered oregano
¼ to ½ teaspoon whole cumin seed (or more for braver souls)
½ to 1 teaspoon chili powder, or to taste

Fantastic Island Soup

This soup recipe is an adaptation of a venerable Danish recipe. It is a cold delight, just right for a hot summer day. It involves no cooking.

Combine buttermilk, tofu, and honey in a blender and process at medium speed.

Beat the eggs until fluffy and add the lemon and vanilla.

Gradually add the buttermilk–tofu mixture to the egg–lemon mixture, beating all the while. Chill. Serve with islands of whipped cream puffs, or with cubes of tofu, or with the following croutons.

3 cups buttermilk
2 cups tofu (about 20 ounces)
4 tablespoons honey
2 eggs
juice of 1 large lemon
grated rind of 1 lemon
2 teaspoons vanilla extract

CROUTONS

Melt the butter in a skillet. Sauté the cubes over a low flame, stirring constantly until browned.

1 cup dried whole wheat bread cubes
2 tablespoons butter (no substitutions)

In small pieces
> zucchini
> summer squash
> broccoli
> carrots
> beets
> onions
> cauliflower
> green beans
> peas
> cabbage or lettuce
> tomatoes
> purple cabbage
> avocado
> corn

12 ounces of firm (pressed)
> tofu

your favorite salad
> dressing

Things you might want to add
> cooked garbanzo
> > beans
> cooked kidney beans
> cooked soybeans
> sprouts
> sunflower seeds or
> > any other seeds or
> > nuts

Tofu Toybox

This is a colorful salad that you'll especially enjoy making with vegetables from your own garden.

Use vegetables that are available to you or that are in season, and be sure to add in any of your own special favorites we might not have mentioned.

Mix the vegetables all together in a bowl, and add any beans or nuts that you would like. Cut the tofu into small pieces, and stir them into the vegetables. Top with dressing, mix well, and place in the refrigerator until supper is ready.

Ms. Muffett Soup

Sauté the vegetables in the butter over low heat. Add the whey and spices and any cooked vegetables you have left over. Serve with tofu curds or cubes of tofu.

Serve the soup with whole grain bread or crackers or okara muffins.

1 small onion, chopped
½ cup celery, chopped
1 small clove garlic, chopped or pressed
¼ cup fresh parsley, chopped
pepper, to taste
pinch of nutmeg
3 cups of whey, with curds
3 tablespoons butter (use only butter here)
1 cup cooked vegetables

Whey Soup

Heat the whey, float the tofu, add the soy sauce, and eat it up.
Yield: 1 serving

1 cup fresh whey
1 large fresh tofu curd
1 teaspoon soy sauce

Carrot and Tofu Salad

Grate a carrot, but not your fingers. Mash some tofu. Mix in lemon juice to taste. Add raisins if you like.

carrot
tofu
lemon juice
raisins

Red, White, and Brown Rounds

Cut a circle of bread with a cookie cutter or a glass rim, and toast. Spread with peanut butter. Top with a cube or a slice of tofu. Balance a strawberry or ½ teaspoon of jelly on top.

whole wheat bread
peanut butter
tofu
strawberry or jelly

Tofu Smoothie

½ cup tofu
½ large banana or 1 whole
   small banana
1 teaspoon lemon juice
1 tablespoon honey
¼ to ½ cup yogurt

Add fruit as you wish
   1 fresh peach
   2 large or 3 small
     plums
   2 large or 3 small
     apricots
   ½ cup berries
   1 peeled apple
   ¼ to ½ cup frozen
     fruit
   ¼ to ½ cup preserved
     fruit

This is a special hot weather treat; children love them and they are substantial enough for a light lunch when served with whole grain cookies.

Blend together the tofu, banana, lemon juice, honey, and yogurt, adding whey or water to thin if necessary.

Add the fruit to the blended mixture and process until it is very smooth. If your blender is strong enough, add some cracked ice.

Serve in a tall, frosted glass. Dust the top with cinnamon.
Yield: 2   8-ounce servings

Soy Shake

½ cup cold soymilk
1 egg
juice from 1 orange
1 tablespoon carob powder
1 tablespoon honey

Whirl together all the ingredients in a blender until they are smooth.

Coconut Mothballs

¼ cup coconut
3 tablespoons honey
½ teaspoon vanilla extract
tofu
wheat germ

Take some shredded coconut. Mix in a bit of honey and vanilla and then enough tofu and wheat germ to make it all stay together. Drop by spoonsful onto a plate and freeze.

166

Old Cake Cookies

A very easy, handy way to make use of stale pieces of leftover cake. Even brown bread will work with good results.

Take some leftover cake, and turn it into lots of crumbs. Mix them with some crumbled tofu and honey, taking little tastes to find out the best amount of each. Roll into balls, then roll the balls in chopped nuts or shredded coconut and chill.

(One cup cake crumbs, plus ¼ cup tofu, plus 2 or 3 tablespoons of honey will make a dozen or so 1-inch balls.)

old cake
tofu
honey
chopped nuts
shredded coconut

Frisbee® Cookies

Preheat oven to 375°F.

You can also make these carob cookies in the regular way and size, but it's a lot more fun to make them huge and call them Frisbee cookies. No throwing, though!

Cream together butter and honey so they are blended well. Add in the beaten eggs. Add the rest of the ingredients and stir together well.

Drop by spoonsful or Frisbeesful onto a lightly oiled cookie sheet and bake for 10 to 12 minutes. Larger cookies may have to stay in a bit longer.

Yield: 1 to 4 dozen cookies, depending on their size

1 cup butter
¾ cup honey
2 eggs, beaten
1¾ cups whole wheat flour
½ cup okara
½ cup carob powder
1 teaspoon baking powder
½ teaspoon baking soda
1 tablespoon vanilla
  extract
1 cup walnuts, chopped
1 cup shredded coconut
(¾ cup raisins—optional)

Michelle's Mud Pies

½ cup peanut butter
¼ cup carob powder
¼ cup okara
⅓ cup honey
¼ cup skimmed milk
   powder

Your choice of
   shredded coconut
   your favorite dried
     fruit
   your favorite nuts
   your favorite seeds
   raisins

Have you ever made a mud pie that you could eat? Well, you won't *really* be using mud in these, but carob powder. You don't have to tell anyone that—let them think it's mud.

Mix together peanut butter, carob, okara, honey, and milk powder, getting out all of the lumps.

Add about ¼ cup of a mixture of two of your favorite nuts, seeds, or fruit, or a couple of tablespoons each of several of them.

If the mud pie batter is too thick to stay together well, add some hot whey or water to make it stickier. Then divide the dough into balls about the size of walnuts and press or pat them into pie-shaped patties on a cookie sheet. Place in the refrigerator until hard.

You can also sprinkle nuts or seeds or wheat germ and such on top of each mud pie. (You can say this is sand, and that it will go well with the mud.)

Yield: 2 dozen pies

Baby Cereal

1 cup cooked oatmeal or
   barley
6 tablespoons cooked
   brown rice
2 tablespoons tofu
milk as needed, either
   formula or prepared for
   baby use

This recipe is suitable for an infant's first cereal.

Place all ingredients in a blender and process until smooth, adding only enough milk to get the consistency you want.

Cereals do not freeze well and should be prepared only as needed for one day's use.

Baby Stew or Soup

Combine all the ingredients in a pot and simmer until they all are well cooked. The water should cover the ingredients.

When cooked, cool and pour the mixture into a blender with tofu–rice mixture in the proportion of ¼ to ½ cup to each cup of cooked stew. Adding more water makes a soup of the stew. Blend until the mixture is very smooth.

Store the prepared stew or soup in the freezer either as cubes made in an ice cube tray, or in separate portions packed in plastic sandwich bags or small paper cups. You can then remove the portions from the freezer as needed and reheat them.

2 carrots
1 zucchini squash
6 or so string beans
¼ cup shelled peas
1 medium potato
1 stalk celery

Add as you wish
- ½ chicken breast, or other chicken in like amount
- ⅓ cup lean beef
- ⅓ cup bone-free fish

water
Baby Cereal (see preceding page) to be added after above ingredients have been cooked

Baby Vegetable

It is best to avoid certain vegetables for very young babies: aromatics such as onion and garlic and vegetables of the cabbage family. Combinations of vegetables are excellent, such as carrots and yellow squash, peas and green beans, beets and carrots, and of course there's the old standby, carrots and peas.

Combine all the ingredients in a blender and process until smooth.

A larger quantity can be frozen. You can provide yourself with a cafeteria of baby foods to choose from, but it's best to have no more than about 10 days' supply ahead, and be sure to date batches. Foods will lose nutrients and quality over a long stay in the freezer.

1 cup cooked vegetable
¼ to ½ cup Baby Cereal (page 168)
water only as needed

169

Baby Fruit

1 cup cooked fruit
¼ to ½ cup Baby Cereal
   (page 168)
honey as needed

Any fruits can be prepared for babies, but the best for very young babies are apples cooked into sauce, and mashed bananas. Other cooked fruits such as peaches, pears, and apricots, can be prepared for slightly older infants, used singly or combined.

Process all ingredients in a blender until smooth. If the cooked fruit is presweetened, do not add sweetener; if not, add only enough to cut extreme tartness—the less sweetener, the better.

Fruit can be stored frozen for only a limited period, or it will lose flavor and nutrients.

Appendices

A   Substituting flours

We don't mean to bind you to using a particular flour, and offer this list of equivalents for 1 cup of all-purpose flour. To properly mix flours, sift five or six times. Alternate flours may require up to 2½ teaspoons of baking powder per cup for optimum leavening. When baking, these flours may do best in a slow oven (300° to 325°F) over a long period.

The following may be substituted for *1 cup of all-purpose flour:*

1¼ cups barley flour
⅞ cup whole wheat flour (14 tablespoons)
1 cup corn flour
1 scant cup fine cornmeal
¾ cup coarse cornmeal
¾ cup potato flour
⅞ cup rice flour
1¼ cups rye flour
1 cup rye meal
1⅓ cups soy flour
1 cup tapioca flour
1⅓ cups ground rolled oats

171

B   Composition of spices*

Blend your own spices, and you can alter the ingredients to suit your tastes. Homemade spices will be fresher, too.

Pumpkin pie spice	(%)
Cinnamon	40
Ginger	20
Nutmeg	20
Allspice	10
Cloves	10

Chili powder	(%)
Red pepper	83
Cumin	9
Oregano	4
Salt	2.5
Garlic powder	1.5

Curry powder	(%)
Coriander	36
Tumeric	28
Cumin	10
Fenugreek seed	10
White pepper	5
Yellow mustard	3
Red pepper	2
Allspice	4
Ginger	2

Poultry seasoning	(%)
White pepper	35
Sage	15
Thyme	10
Marjoram	10
Savory	10
Ginger	10
Allspice	5
Nutmeg	5

*U.S. Department of Agriculture; Composition of Foods: Spices and Herbs (Raw • Processed • Prepared); prepared by Marsh, Anne C.; Moss, Mary K; and Murphy, Elizabeth W. Handbook no. 8-2. (Washington, D.C.: Government Printing Office, revised January 1977).

C   *Miscellaneous substitutions*

1 tablespoon carob powder	1 tablespoon cocoa
3 tablespoons cocoa + 1½ teaspoons fat	1 ounce (square) carob
1 teaspoon baking powder	¼ teaspoon baking soda + ½ teaspoon cream of tartar

1 cup milk	1 cup soymilk
1 cup milk	1 cup evaporated milk + ½ cup water
1 cup sour cream	⅓ cup butter + ⅔ cup milk
1 cup buttermilk	⅞ cup milk + 2 tablespoons white vinegar

To thicken:	*Wheat flour*
1½ teaspoons potato flour	1 tablespoon
2 teaspoons arrowroot	1¾ tablespoons
1 tablespoon cornstarch	2 tablespoons
2 teaspoons rice flour	1¾ tablespoons
1 teaspoon barley flour	2 teaspoons

D *Table of equivalents*

a pinch, a dash, or a few grains	slightly less than ⅛ teaspoon
60 drops	1 teaspoon
3 teaspoons	1 tablespoon
4 tablespoons	¼ cup
2 tablespoons	1 ounce (liquid)
1 cup (liquid)	½ pint
4 cups (liquid)	1 quart
4 quarts	1 gallon
2 cups (liquid)	16 ounces
1 stick butter	½ cup, ¼ pound
1 cup tofu	10 ounces
1 cup grated cheese	¼ pound
1 cup rice, uncooked	2 cups, cooked
¼ cup lemon juice	juice of 1 lemon
¼ cup lime juice	juice of 2 limes

E   Fahrenheit and Celsius equivalents

very slow	250° to 275°F	121° to 132°C
slow oven	300° to 325°F	149° to 162°C
moderate oven	350° to 375°F	176° to 190°C
hot (quick)	400° to 450°F	204° to 232°C
very hot	475° up	246°C up
broil	550°F	288°C
boiling	212°F	100°C
(sea level)		
freezing	32°F	0°C

F Recommended daily dietary allowances[a]

	Age (yrs.)	Weight (lbs.)	Weight (kg.)	Height (in.)	Height (cm.)	Energy (kcal.)[b]	Protein (gr.)	Vitamin A activity (RE)[c]	Vitamin A activity (I.U.)	Vitamin D (I.U.)	Vitamin E activity[d] (I.U.)
Infants	0.0–0.5	14	6	24	60	kg. × 117	kg. × 2.2	420	1,400	400	4
	0.5–1.0	20	9	28	71	kg. × 108	kg. × 2.0	400	2,000	400	5
Children	1–3	28	13	34	86	1,300	23	400	2,000	400	7
	4–6	44	20	44	110	1,800	30	500	2,500	400	9
	7–10	66	30	54	135	2,400	36	700	3,300	400	10
Males	11–14	97	44	63	158	2,800	44	1,000	5,000	400	12
	15–18	134	61	69	172	3,000	54	1,000	5,000	400	15
	19–22	147	67	69	172	3,000	54	1,000	5,000	400	15
	23–50	154	70	69	172	2,700	56	1,000	5,000		15
	51+	154	70	69	172	2,400	56	1,000	5,000		15
Females	11–14	97	44	62	155	2,400	44	800	4,000	400	12
	15–18	119	54	65	162	2,100	48	800	4,000	400	12
	19–22	128	58	65	162	2,100	46	800	4,000	400	12
	23–50	128	58	65	162	2,000	46	800	4,000		12
	51+	128	58	65	162	1,800	46	800	4,000		12
Pregnant						+300	+30	1,000	5,000	400	15
Lactating						+500	+20	1,200	6,000	400	15

[a]The allowances are intended to provide for individual variations among most normal persons as they live in the United States under usual environmental stresses.

[b]Kilojoules (kJ) = 4.2 × kcal.

[c]Retinol equivalents.

[d]Total vitamin E activity, estimated to be 80 percent as α-tocopherol and 20 percent other tocopherols.

Water-soluble vitamins							Minerals					
Ascor-bic acid (mg.)	Fola-cin[e] (μg)	Nia-cin[f] (mg.)	Ribo-flavin (mg.)	Thia-mine (mg.)	Vita-min B_6 (mg.)	Vita-min B_{12} (μg)	Cal-cium (mg.)	Phos-phorus (mg.)	Iodine (μg)	Iron (mg.)	Mag-nesium (mg.)	Zinc (mg.)
35	50	5	0.4	0.3	0.3	0.3	360	240	35	10	60	3
35	50	8	0.6	0.5	0.4	0.3	540	400	45	15	70	5
40	100	9	0.8	0.7	0.6	1.0	800	800	60	15	150	10
40	200	12	1.1	0.9	0.9	1.5	800	800	80	10	200	10
40	300	16	1.2	1.2	1.2	2.0	800	800	110	10	250	10
45	400	18	1.5	1.4	1.6	3.0	1,200	1,200	130	18	350	15
45	400	20	1.8	1.5	2.0	3.0	1,200	1,200	150	18	400	15
45	400	20	1.8	1.5	2.0	3.0	800	800	140	10	350	15
45	400	18	1.6	1.4	2.0	3.0	800	800	130	10	350	15
45	400	16	1.5	1.2	2.0	3.0	800	800	110	10	350	15
45	400	16	1.3	1.2	1.6	3.0	1,200	1,200	115	18	300	15
45	400	14	1.4	1.1	2.0	3.0	1,200	1,200	115	18	300	15
45	400	14	1.4	1.1	2.0	3.0	800	800	100	18	300	15
45	400	13	1.2	1.0	2.0	3.0	800	800	100	18	300	15
45	400	12	1.1	1.0	2.0	3.0	800	800	80	10	300	15
60	800	+2	+0.3	+0.3	2.5	4.0	1,200	1,200	125	18+[g]	450	20
80	600	+4	+0.5	+0.3	2.5	4.0	1,200	1,200	150	18	450	25

[e]The folacin allowances refer to dietary sources as determined by *Lactobacillus casei* assay. Pure forms of folacin may be effective in doses less than one-fourth of the recommended dietary allowance.

[f]Although allowances are expressed as niacin, it is recognized that, on the average, 1 mg. of niacin is derived from each 60 mg. of dietary tryptophan.

[g]This increased requirement cannot be met by ordinary diets; therefore, the use of supplemental iron is recommended.

(Compiled by the Food and Nutrition Board, National Academy of Sciences—National Research Council, revised 1974)

Index

A

Additives, lack of, in tofu, 2–3
Æbleskiver, 142
Almond filling, for kuchen, 114
Almond–vegetable–tofu sauté, 67
Amino acids, essential, in tofu, 6–7
Anadama bread, 117
Apricot hard sauce, 154
Artichoke casserole, tofu, 54
Austrian dip or spread, 137

B

Baby food
    cereal, 168
    fruit, 170
    stew or soup, 169
    vegetable, 169

Baked stuffed zucchini, 47–48
Banana–coconut–tofu bread, 120
Banana okara bread, 33, 120
Batter, for deep frying, 87
Bavarian cream, 154
Bean curd, 1. *See also* Tofu
Bearnaise sauce, tofu, 132
Biscuits, okara bran, 123
Blueberry cake, okara, 160
Blue cheese dressing, tofu, 107
Blue cheese spread, 139
Borscht, Ukranian, 97
Bran biscuits, okara, 123
Brandteigkrapfer mit salziger
    fulle, 88
Bread
    anadama, 117
    banana–coconut–tofu, 120
    banana–okara, 33, 120
    casserole dill, 121
    fruit, 119

Irish soda, 117
Nellie Twomey's soda, 118
okara flatbread, 126
orange nut, 115
peasant, 116
pumpkin spice, 119
sourdough health, 115
whole wheat, 114
Bread sticks, rye, 111
Breakfasts
æbleskiver, 142
cornmeal cereal, 146
dieter's pancakes, 144
French toast, 147
Klondike pancakes, 141
okara oatmeal, 33
okara sausage patties, 148
okara sourdough pancakes
and waffles, 143
okara whole wheat waffles,
144
Persian pancakes, 141
rice flour–okara waffles, 145
risengrød, 147
scrambled tofu, 145
Broccoli casserole, tofu, 51
Broiled tofu slices, 48
Broth, chicken, 98
Brownies, fudge, 156
Bulgur salad, 103
Buns
Chinese steamed, 85
sesame whole wheat, 114
Burgers, PSP, 79
Buttermilk doughnuts, 124
Buttermilk kuchen, 113
B vitamins, in whey, 8, 31

C

Cabbage leaves, preparing for
stuffing, 81
Cabbage–potato–tofu casserole,
53
Cabbage rolls, stuffed, 75
Cake
buttermilk kuchen, 113
coffee, 113
okara blueberry, 160
okara carrot, 159
quick coffee, 121
Cake toppings, 122
Calcium
in soymilk, 35, 37
in tofu, 8, 15
Calcium chloride, 5, 15
Calcium sulfate, 5, 8, 15
Calories
quantities of, comparing
tofu, cheese, and beef, 2
recommended daily intake
of, 26
Carbohydrates, in okara, 8
Carob shake concentrate, 40
Carrot cake, okara, 159
Carrot tofu loaf, 56
with PSP, 76–77
Carrots Parmesan, with tofu, 57
Carrot and tofu salad, for children, 165
Casserole dill bread, 121
Casseroles
eggplant Italienne, 52
potato–tofu–cabbage, 53
tofu artichoke with chicken
or tuna, 54
tofu broccoli, 51
tortilla, 55
Cereal
baby, 168
cornmeal, 146
hot okara oatmeal, 33
rice cooked in milk, 147–48
Cheese ball, tofu, 88

Cheese pie
    Greek, 84
    tofu, 150
Cheese rarebit, 51
Cheese and tofu sandwich,
    grilled, 100
Cheese torte, tofu, 152
Chicken, tofu artichoke casserole
    with, 54
Chicken soup or broth, 98
Children's dishes, 163–68
    carrot and tofu salad, 165
    coconut mothballs, 166
    fantastic island soup, 163
    Frisbee cookies, 167
    glorious mess, 163
    Michelle's mud pies, 168
    Ms. Muffet soup, 165
    old cake cookies, 167
    red, white, and brown
        rounds, 165
    soy shake, 166
    tofu smoothie, 166
    tofu toybox, 164
    whey soup, 165
Chili, meatless, 57
Chili con PSP, 77
Chinese steamed buns, 85
Chowder, clam, with PSP, 98
Clam chowder, with PSP, 98
Coating, okara fry-and-bake, 87
Coconut mothballs, for children,
    166
Coffee cake, 113
    quick, 121
Complementary foods, for com-
    plete protein intake, 6–8
Cookies
    Frisbee, 167
    oatmeal okara, 156
    old cake, 167
    zucchini, 157

Cornmeal cereal, 146
Cornsticks, okara, 123
Corn and tofu soufflé, 59
Cost, of tofu, 2, 5–6
Crackers
    oatmeal with tofu, 124–25
    tofu okara, 125–26
Cream, Bavarian, 154
Cream cheese, tofu, 138
Cream soup, basic, 97
Creamy tofu mustard sauce, 133
Creme, Spanish, 155
Croquettes, okara meat, 69
Croutons, 163
Cucumber sandwich spread, 138
Curdling agents. See Solidifiers
Curry, Indian, 62
Curry patties, okara–
    mushroom–shrimp, 66
Curry sauce, 134
Custard, soy, baked, 153–54

D

Dairy foods, tofu substituted for,
    2
Deep-fried sesame tofu, 49
Deep frying, batter for, 87
Desserts, 150–60
    list of, 149
Dieter's pancakes, 144
Dieting, tofu and, 25–26
Digestion, of tofu, 2
Dinner loaf with PSP, 74
Dip
    Austrian, 137
    tofu base, 136
    for tofu cubes, 135
    tofu ghenouj, 137
    for vegetables, 136
Dough
    okara Danish yeast, 112

pizza, with okara, 82
for wonton or pot stickers, 91
Doughnuts, buttermilk, 124
Dow-foo chow yoke, 68
Dressing. *See* Salad dressing
Dumplings
fruit, 159
okara turkey, 85

E

Eggless lemon pie, 151
Eggnog mousse, 154
Egg noodles, whole wheat, 91
Eggplant casserole Italienne, 52
Egg roll, 90
Eggs
okara substituted for, 31
tofu substituted for, 25–26
Egg salad, tofu, 103
Enchiladas, tofu, 63
Enchilada sauce, 63
quantity, 64
English muffins, 111
Epsom salt, as solidifier, 14
Essential amino acids, in tofu,
6–7
Expense. *See* Cost

F

Fantastic island soup, for chil-
dren, 163
Fermented milk. *See* Koumiss
Fiber, from okara, 8, 29–30, 31
Filled puffs, 88
Filling
almond, for kuchen, 114
for pancakes, 142
Fish-flavored sauce, 134
Flatbread, okara, 126
Flavor, of tofu, 3, 22

Flavoring, for processed soy pro-
tein, 42
Freezing, of tofu, 23–24
French dressing, 107
French toast, 147
Freshness. *See also* Storing
restoring to tofu, 23
Frisbee cookies, 167
Fruit, for babies, 170
Fruit bread, 119
Fruit dumplings, 159
Fry-and-bake coating, okara, 87
Frying, deep, batter, 87
Fudge brownies, 156

G

Garbanzo okara loaf, 55
Gazpacho, 99
Glorious mess, for children, 163
Granola, 34
Grape leaves, stuffed, 80, 81
Greek cheese pie, 84
Green goddess dressing, 108
Green peppers stuffed with tofu,
72
Grilled cheese and tofu sand-
wich, 100
Gypsum. *See* Calcium sulfate

H

Hazelnut okara torte, 153
Hollandaise sauce, tofu, 131
Honey syrup, 142
Hot cereal, okara oatmeal, 33
Hot tofu tuna salad, 58

I

Indian curry, 62
Irish soda bread, 117
Iron, in tofu, 8

J

Japanese-style meatballs, 79

K

Kids' foods. *See* Baby food; Children's dishes
Kima, 62
Klondike pancakes, 141
Koumiss, 39–40
    soy, 40
Kreplach, 84
Kuo teh, 92

L

Land use, efficiency of, with tofu, 3, 6
Lasagna, tofu, 47
Leaves, preparing for stuffing, 81
Lemon juice, as curdling agent, 15
Lemon pie, eggless, 151
Lentil stew, 62
Lettuce leaves, preparing for stuffing, 81
Liptauer, 137
Loaf
    carrot tofu, 56
        with PSP, 76
    dinner, with PSP, 74
    garbanzo okara, 55
    tofu meat, 56
Low-calorie Thousand Island dressing, 108

M

Macaroons, okara and coconut, 157
Magnesium chloride, 5, 15

Magnesium content, of tofu, 15
Main dishes, 45–82
    list of, 45–46
Mayonnaise, tofu, 105
Meatballs, Japanese-style, 79
Meat croquettes, okara, 69
Meat extender, okara as, 30
Meatless chili, 57
Meat loaf, tofu, 56
Michelle's mud pies, for children, 168
Milkshakes, with soymilk, 39
    carob concentrate for, 40
    peach, 39
    soy shake, 166
Minerals, in tofu, 8–9
Minestrone, 96
Mold, to press tofu, 13–14
Mousse
    basic, 155
    eggnog, 154
Ms. Muffet soup, for children, 165
Muffins, English, 111
Mugs' and Kate's pincushion rolls, 112
Mushroom–okara–shrimp curry patties, 66
Mushrooms à la creme tofu, 64
Mustard sauce, creamy tofu, 133

N

Nellie Twomey's soda bread, 118
Newburg, tofu à la, 66
Nigari, 5, 8
Noodles
    egg, whole wheat, 91
    Romanov tofu, 67
Nut bread, orange, 115
Nutrition, tofu and, 6–9

O

Oatmeal, okara and, 33
Oatmeal crackers, with tofu, 124–25
Oatmeal okara cookies, 156
Okara, 3, 29–31
    baking with, 111–26
    as by-product of tofu, 18
    granola with, 34
    nutritional content of, 8
    recipe list, 32
    storing, 31
    uses for, 28, 30–31
Okara blueberry cake, 160
Okara bran biscuits, 123
Okara bread, banana, 33
Okara carrot cake, 159
Okara and coconut macaroons, 157
Okara cornsticks, 123
Okara Danish yeast dough, 112
Okara flatbread, 126
Okara fry-and-bake coating, 87
Okara loaf, garbanzo, 55
Okara meat croquettes, 69
Okara–mushroom–shrimp curry patties, 66
Okara oatmeal hot cereal, 33
Okara patties, 32
Okara pizza dough, 82
Okara sausage patties, 148
Okara sourdough pancakes and waffles, 143
Okara stuffing, for poultry, 86
Okara tofu spice bars, 158
Okara turkey dumplings, 85
Okara whole wheat waffles, 144
Okara zucchini soufflé, 61
Old cake cookies, for children, 167
Orange nut bread, 115

Oriental salad, 104
    dressing for, 105

P

Pancakes
    Danish, 142
    dieter's, 144
    Klondike, 141
    okara sourdough, 143
    Persian, 141–42
Pao-tze, 85
Papaya leaves, preparing for stuffing, 81
Parsley sauce, 130
Patties
    okara, 32
    okara–mushroom–shrimp curry, 66
    okara sausage, 148
Peach milkshake, 39
Peasant bread, 116
Peppers, green, stuffed with tofu, 72
Persian pancakes, 141–42
Pesto sauce, 50
Pie
    eggless lemon, 151
    Greek cheese, 84
    Michelle's mud, 168
    tamale, 68–69
    tofu cheese, 150
    yogurt, 151
Pierogi, 84
Pie shell
    for quiche, 71
    sweet, 152
Pizza dough, with okara, 82
Pizza sauce, 82
Popcorn, spiked, 90

Potassium, in tofu, 8
Potatoes, rebaked, with tofu, 89
Potato salad, Uncle Perk's, 102
Potato soup, vegetarian, 99
Potato–tofu–cabbage casserole, 53
Pot stickers, 92
    dough for, 91
Poultry, okara stuffing for, 86
Preservatives, in tofu, 2, 5
Pressing, of tofu, 19. *See also* Mold
Pressing sack, 13
Price. *See* Cost
Processed soy protein. *See* PSP
Protein
    availability of, in tofu, 6–8
    quantities of, comparing tofu, cheese, and beef, 1–2
    recommended daily intake of, 26
    in soy sprouts, 9
    unavailability of, in raw soybeans, 9, 17
Protein complementarity, 6–8
PSP, 23–24, 41–43
    carrot tofu loaf with, 76–77
    chili con, 77
    clam chowder with, 98
    dinner loaf with, 74
    making, 41–42
        dry method, 73
        wet method, 73
    recipe list, 43
    skillet supper with, 80
    storing, 42
PSP burgers, 79
PSP sloppy joes, 74
PSP snack, 86
PSP stroganoff, 78
Puffs, filled, 88
Pumpkin spice bread, 119

Quiche
    pie shell for, 71
    tofu, 70
    vegetable, 71
Quick coffee cake, 121

R

Rarebit, cheese, 51
Ravioli, 50
Rebaked potatoes with tofu, 89
Red, white, and brown rounds, 165
Rice, cooked in milk with okara, 147–48
Rice flour–okara waffles, 145
Risengrød, 147–48
Rolls, Mugs' and Kate's pincushion, 112
Roughage. *See* Fiber
Rye bread sticks, 111

S

Salad
    carrot and tofu, 165
    Oriental, 104
    spinach, 104
    sweet and sour, 102
    tabouli (bulgur), 103
    tofu–egg, 103
    Uncle Perk's potato, 102
    Waldorf, 101
Salad dressing
    French, 107
    green goddess, 108
    low-calorie Thousand Island, 108
    for Oriental salad, 104

tarragon tofu, 106
tofu–blue cheese, 107
tofu extraordinaire, 106
tofu mayonnaise, 105
tofu tahini, 107
tomato, 106
Waldorf, 101
Salt, use of, 44
Sandwich
grilled cheese and tofu, 100
red, white, and brown
rounds, 165
Tia's tofu, 101
tofu in, 100
tofu tuna salad, 100
Sandwich spread. *See* Spread
Sauce
apricot hard, 154
creamy tofu mustard, 133
curry, 134
for dipping, 135
enchilada, 63, 64
fish-flavored, 134
parsley, 130
pesto, 50
pizza, 82
spaghetti, 78
sweet-and-sour, 49
sweet yogurt, 133
tofu bearnaise, 132
tofu hollandaise, 131
tomato, 133
white, 129–30
ymer, 132
Sausage patties, okara, 148
Sauté, almond–vegetable–tofu,
67
Scones, with okara, 122
Scrambled tofu, 145–46
Seafood spread, 139
Sesame buns, whole wheat, 114
Sesame tofu, deep-fried, 49

Settling cloth, 13
Shrimp–mushroom–okara curry
patties, 66
Shrimp and tofu, 65
Side dishes and preparations,
83–93
recipe list, 83
Skillet supper, 80
Sloppy joes, with PSP, 74
Snack, with PSP, 86
Soda bread
Irish, 117
Nellie Twomey's, 118
Solidifiers, 5, 8, 14–15
how to use, 18–19
Soufflé
corn and tuna, 59
okara zucchini, 61
spinach, 60
vegetable, 60
Soup
for babies, 169
chicken, 98
clam chowder with PSP, 98
cream, 97
fantastic island, 163
gazpacho, 99
minestrone, 96
Ms. Muffet, 165
Ukranian borscht, 97
vegetarian potato, 99
whey, 165
Sourdough health bread, 115
Sourdough pancakes and waffles, 143
Sourdough starter, 116
Soybeans
chemical additives in, 2–3
growing, 9–11
nutritional value when
cooked or sprouted, 9
yield of tofu per pound of, 6

Soy cheese, 1. *See also* Tofu
Soy custard, baked, 153–54
Soy koumiss, 40
Soymilk, 4
    as by-product of tofu, 17–18
    fortification of, 37
    freezing of, 37
    making, 36–38
    milkshakes with, 39–40
    nutritional value of, 35
    recipe list, 36
    as substitute for dairy milk,
      2, 35
    uses for, 28
Soy shake, 66
Soy sprouts, 9
Spaghetti sauce, 78
Spanish creme, 155
Spice bars, okara tofu, 158
Spice bread, pumpkin, 119
Spiked popcorn, 90
Spinach salad, 104
Spinach soufflé, 60
Spread
    Austrian, 137
    blue cheese, 139
    cucumber sandwich, 138
    seafood, 139
    tofu cream cheese, 138
Sprouted soybeans. *See* Soy
    sprouts
Stew
    for babies, 169
    lentil, 61
Stir-fried tofu, 68
Stock, for cooking cabbage rolls,
    75
Storing
    PSP, 42
    tofu, 19, 22
      freezing, 23–24
Stroganoff, PSP, 78

Stuffed cabbage rolls, 75
Stuffed grape leaves, 80
Stuffed peppers, 72
Stuffed zucchini, baked, 47–48
Stuffing, okara, for poultry, 86
Sugars, natural, in whey, 8, 31
Sweet pie shell, 152
Sweet and sour salad, 102
Sweet-and-sour sauce, 49
Sweet yogurt sauce, 133
Syrup
    carob, for milkshakes, 40
    honey, 142

T

Tabouli, 103
Tacos, 76
Tamale pie, 68–69
Tarragon tofu dressing, 106
Taste. *See* Flavor
Textured Vegetable Protein, 24,
    41
Thousand Island dressing, low-
    calorie, 108
Tia's tofu sandwich, 101
Tiropeta, 84
Tofu
    advantages of, 1–4, 5–9
      cost, 2, 5–6
      digestion, 2
      efficiency of land use, 3
      lack of chemical additives,
        2–3
    Carrots Parmesan with, 57
    deep-fried sesame, 49
    green peppers stuffed with,
      72
    making, 12–21
      in quantity, 10–21

mineral content of, 8–9
okara from, 3
protein content of, 1–2, 6–8
rebaked potatoes with, 89
restoring freshness of, 23
in sandwiches, 100–101
scrambled, 145–46
shrimp and, 67
soymilk from, 4
stir-fried, 68
storing, 18, 22
    freezing, 23–24
as substitute for dairy foods, 2
as substitute for eggs, 25–26
taste of, 3
uses for, 24, 26–28
vegetarians and, 24–25
weight control and, 25–26
whey from, 3–4
yield of per pound of soy-
    beans, 6
Tofu–almond–vegetable sauté, 67
Tofu artichoke casserole with
    chicken or tuna, 54
Tofu bearnaise sauce, 132
Tofu–blue cheese dressing, 107
Tofu broccoli casserole, 51
Tofu casserole, tuna, 53
Tofu cheese ball, 88
Tofu cheese pie, 150
Tofu cheese torte, 152
Tofu cream cheese, 138
Tofu dip base, 136
Tofu dressing, 106
Tofu–egg salad, 103
Tofu enchiladas, 63
Tofu ghenouj, 137
Tofu hollandaise sauce, 131
Tofu lasagna, 47
Tofu loaf, carrot, 56
    with PSP, 76–77

Tofu mayonnaise, 105
Tofu meat loaf, 56
Tofu à la Newburg, 66
Tofu noodles Romanov, 67
Tofu okara crackers, 125–26
Tofu–potato–cabbage casserole,
    53
Tofu quiche, 70
Tofu sandwiches, 100–101
Tofu slices, broiled, 48
Tofu smoothie, for children, 166
Tofu soufflé, corn and, 59
Tofu tahini salad dressing, 107
Tofu toybox, for children, 164
Tofu tuna salad, hot, 58
Tofu tuna salad sandwich, 100
Tomato dressing, 106
Tomato sauce, 133
Topping
    for cakes, 122
    for tofu cheese pie, 150
Torte
    hazelnut okara, 153
    tofu cheese, 152
Tortilla casserole, 55
Trypsin inhibitor, 17
Tuna, tofu artichoke casserole
    with, 54
Tuna salad, hot tofu, 58
Tuna salad sandwich, tofu, 100
Tuna tofu casserole, 53
Turkey dumplings, okara, 85
TVP. *See* Textured Vegetable Pro-
    tein

U

Ukranian borscht, 97
Uncle Perk's potato salad, 102

V

Vegans, tofu for, 24–25
Vegetable, for babies, 169
Vegetable–almond–tofu sauté, 67
Vegetable quiche, 71
Vegetable soufflé, 60
Vegetarian potato soup, 99
Vegetarians, tofu for, 24–25
Vinegar, as curdling agent, 15
Vitamin A, in soybeans, 9
Vitamin B complex. *See* B vitamins

Vitamin B_{12}, in soymilk, 35, 37
Vitamin C, in soy sprouts, 9
Vitamin E, in soy sprouts, 9
Vitamin K, in soy sprouts, 9

W

Waffles
    Klondike, 141
    okara sourdough, 143
    okara whole wheat, 144
    rice flour–okara, 145
Waldorf salad, 101
Weight control. *See* Dieting
Whey, 3–4, 31–32
    as by-product of tofu, 18
    nutritional content of, 8–9, 31
    uses for, 28, 32
Whey soup, for children, 165
White sauce, 129–30
Whole wheat egg noodles, 91
Whole wheat sesame buns and bread, 114
Whole wheat waffles, okara, 144
Wonton, 93
    dough for, 91

Υ

Yeast dough, okara Danish, 112
Yiaourtopeta, 151
Ymer, 132
Yogurt pie, 151
Yogurt sauce, sweet, 133

Z

Zucchini, baked stuffed, 47–48
Zucchini cookies, 157
Zucchini entrée squares, 61
Zucchini soufflé, okara, 61